MW01136666

OUR DAILY BREAD

pil

Publications International, Ltd.

Let's get social!
 @Publications_International
 @PublicationsInternational
www.pilbooks.com

CONTENTS

Faith in God transforms our lives. When we open our hearts to God, we see the ways his many blessings flow through us and imbue our lives with love and guidance. Sometimes, however, his grace is more difficult to find. In periods of doubt and anger, God seems distant from us. We feel lost, and it becomes easier to justify our failures and sinfulness. We move further from God, sometimes with sharp defiance, sometimes with apathy. Take comfort in your faith and remember that God will never abandon you. Find his loving presence all around you, in the ground beneath your feet, the warming sun on your face, and the gentle music of his songbirds.

Our Daily Bread is a companion to help you on your life journey by deepening your faith and strengthening your connection to God. Throughout this book, you'll find verses, reflections, prayers, and quotes for every day of the calendar year. From page to page, you'll encounter comfort, wisdom, challenge, and inspiration.

This special devotional book will help you find the thoughts, feelings, and words you wish to convey to God. Whether you are seeking his grace, his mercy, or his love when dealing with the relationships in your life, or you're asking for strength and resilience when life's little detours test your patience, God is right there, waiting to hear from you and give you just what you need to get through the day. While daily entries take only a minute or two to read, the focus of the content is sure to remain with you throughout the day as a source of encouragement.

Spending time each day in prayer will help you refocus your faith, remind you of God's blessings, and recognize his guiding hand. The more you look around with an open heart, the more you will see that God is there to nourish you: body, soul, and spirit.

JANUARY

JANUARY 1

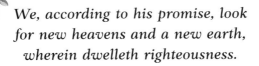

We, according to his promise, look for new heavens and a new earth, wherein dwelleth righteousness.

2 Peter 3:13

As a New Year begins, you may expect new opportunities or different outcomes. Perhaps you are thinking about new habits and setting new goals. These are helpful things to think about. But God has promised something fresher and more transformative. He promises new heavens and a new earth where righteousness prevails. Live your year in light of that. It is comforting, and true.

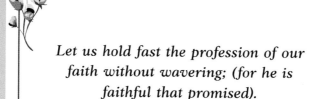

Let us hold fast the profession of our faith without wavering; (for he is faithful that promised).

Hebrews 10:23

Dear God, thank you for giving me a powerful foundation of faith in my life. From this foundation, I am able to build so much peace, harmony, and happiness, just by trusting in you and in your unceasing guidance. I walk in gratitude daily for the miraculous way having faith in your will seems to work. No matter what is going on around me, if I stand in faith, I stand strong. I pray that I always have this trust in your will to depend on, especially when my own will leads me astray. I pray that my life be a testament to others of the wonders that happen when we put our faith in you, God, where it belongs. Amen.

Give us day by day our daily bread.

Luke 11:3

Lord, each day you furnish us with our daily bread. You feed and nourish us, yet often we neglect to acknowledge your gifts of food.

Forgive us, Father, for our selfishness and our disregard for your faithful care. We know that prayer should be a necessary part of every meal.

If, in our haste, we forget to thank you, Lord, remind us of our rudeness. Our meals are not complete until we thank the giver for his many gifts.

And ye shall seek me, and find me,
when ye shall search for me with
all your heart.

Jeremiah 29:13

Lord, how many times have I resolved to
spend time first thing each morning in your
Word and in prayer—and how many times
have I neglected to do so! A day that begins
with you, Lord, is sure to be a day blessed
by you. Give me an insatiable thirst for time
with you, Lord. And thank you for always
being available to meet with me.

JANUARY 5

She is more precious than rubies: and all the things thou canst desire are not to be compared unto her.

Proverbs 3:15

Life can be complicated; in the larger world we are challenged, sometimes on a daily basis, to be our best selves. Perhaps we don't see eye-to-eye with a coworker. Maybe we need to have a talk with a friend who has hurt us, even though we dislike confrontation. Can it be that the sweet, adoring toddler we walked to preschool seemingly yesterday has morphed into a teen who is trying to individuate—but doesn't yet know how to do that in a mature or loving way? Though life's hurts can chip away at our spirits, God reminds us that each of us has value. May we never lose sight of the fact that God created us! May we never lose sight of our inherent worth.

JANUARY 6

And all they that were about them strengthened their hands with vessels of silver, with gold, with goods, and with beasts, and with precious things, beside all that was willingly offered.

Ezra 1:6

School has always been hard for eight-year-old Josie, who struggles academically but also, sometimes, with social cues. Josie has a tutor to help her with the academics, but Josie's mom Lori also knows that little tokens—glittery pencils, a small stuffed toy to fit in a pocket—help encourage her daughter. "I wish school was easier for Josie," Lori says. "But I know there are things I can do to help her navigate her day." Dear God, gifts are excellent tokens that encourage and uplift people. May I remember that such a gesture can do much good.

Blessed be the God and Father of our Lord Jesus Christ, which according to his abundant mercy hath begotten us again unto a lively hope by the resurrection of Jesus Christ from the dead.

1 Peter 1:3

O God of strength, passing all understanding, who mercifully givest to thy people mercy and judgment; grant to us, we beseech thee, faithfully to love thee, and to walk this day in the way of righteousness; through Jesus Christ our Lord. Amen.

—11th-century prayer

JANUARY 8

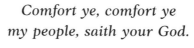

Comfort ye, comfort ye
my people, saith your God.

Isaiah 40:1

Lord, today I ask you to bless and comfort all
who daily see pain and desperation as part
of their jobs. Bless the social workers, Lord,
and comfort them with the knowledge that
what they do truly matters. Bless the doctors
and nurses working with the seriously ill,
and comfort them with your insight. Bless
and comfort the caretakers toiling through
the night, Lord, and send your strength to
restore them. All these people are serving
you as they serve others. Please give them
your special blessing. Amen.

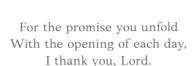

For the promise you unfold
With the opening of each day,
I thank you, Lord.

For blessings shared along the way,
I thank you, Lord.

For the comfort of our home filled
With love to keep us warm,
I thank you, Lord.

For shelter from the winter storm,
I thank you, Lord.

For the gifts of peace and grace you
Grant the family snug within,
I thank you, Lord.

For shielding us from harm and sin,
I thank you, Lord.

For the beauty of the snow
Sparkling in the winter sun,
I thank you, Lord.

For the peace when the day is done,
I thank you, Lord.

Who, when he came, and had seen the grace of God, was glad, and exhorted them all, that with purpose of heart they would cleave unto the Lord.

Acts 11:23

When layoffs hit the company where Christine works, morale fell. "I manage a small staff," Christine explains. "It was up to me to uplift my direct reports during a time when none of us were sure that we'd still have a job when we came to work each morning. I firmly believe God helped me through that chapter." Things have improved for Christine's employer, but she learned something from the experience: "With God's help, I can inspire others." Dear Lord, in Acts we learn about Barnabas, who encouraged early Christians to strengthen their faith even as they were persecuted. Help me to remember that one person can make a difference!

JANUARY 11

But now, O Lord, thou art our father;
we are the clay, and thou our potter;
and we all are the work of thy hand.

Isaiah 64:8

Here we are again, Lord. Another time when
I feel like I've made a complete mess of this
life you've given me. I place myself in your
hands. If you need to totally reshape me to
turn me into someone more useful, so
be it! Thank you for not abandoning me,
your humble creation. Make me
over in your design.

And blessed is she that believed: for there shall be a performance of those things which were told her from the Lord.

Luke 1:45

Our relationships strengthen us. This came home to me the other day, when an exchange with a coworker left me feeling irresolute and unsettled. During my commute home, my stomach was in knots: I went over and over the disagreement in my head. It was hard to sort out whether I'd handled things with grace. When I got home, I found that my husband had started dinner; the warm atmosphere of love and regard unclenched my heart, and I was able to talk frankly about the day. My husband's nonjudgmental but clear-sighted perspective helped me sort how to remedy the situation; after we talked, we took a moment to pray together. God, thank you for reminding us of the importance of believing: in you, and in one another.

The Lord is nigh unto them that are of a broken heart; and saveth such as be of a contrite spirit.

Psalm 34:18

I am like two halves of a walnut, God. I am of two minds: despairing and hopeful. Help me to feel your hand holding me together as I rebuild my life when at first it seemed too hard to even try. In order to get to the meat of a walnut, it must be split into halves. May the brokenness I feel get me to the nourishment—the meat—I need in order to move on. Amen.

But Moses hands were heavy; and they took a stone, and put it under him, and he sat thereon; and Aaron and Hur stayed up his hands, the one on the one side, and the other on the other side; and his hands were steady until the going down of the sun.

Exodus 17:12

Though Meg's mom is wheelchair-bound, she's still game for adventure. And Meg, at 60, is grateful she still has the strength to take her mom out. "It can be a big production," Meg says. "It'll be snowing, and getting my mom in and out of the car with the chair can be tiring. But I'm glad I can still do it: we go out for coffee at our favorite diner, or we'll go shopping together. It's always worth it!" God, sometimes uplifting others means offering actual physical help. Please grant me the literal strength to be able to do so!

For the earth shall be filled with the knowledge of the glory of the Lord, as the waters cover the sea.

Habakkuk 2:14

O Lord, how magnificent is your work on this earth. We can stand at the seashore and feel our own souls rising and filling with your majesty as we marvel at the tides. Or we can walk down a trail and notice that each and every twig has been frosted individually with more icy flakes than we can imagine. We praise you for this awesome creation you share with us, Lord. The more we see of it, the more amazed we are. To you be the glory!

*Come unto me, all ye that labour
and are heavy laden,
and I will give you rest.*

Matthew 11:28

O God, I know you will never give us a
burden to bear without giving us the grace
to endure it, but some burdens just seem
so heavy we find ourselves wondering if
they can be survived. I ask that you send
an abundant amount of strength and grace
to all those who suffer so. Let them feel
your presence in a very real way, Lord, for
without you, they have no hope. I ask this in
Jesus' name. Amen.

JANUARY 17

And be not conformed to this world: but be ye transformed by the renewing of your mind, that ye may prove what is that good, and acceptable, and perfect, will of God.

Romans 12:2

Guide us, dear God, to the perfect destiny you have set out for us. Help keep us on the path to right action, right choices, and right solutions to the problems we may encounter. Help deliver us from obstacles that may detour us and lead us astray. Show us the way to fulfill your divine plan.

With good will doing service, as to the Lord, and not to men.

Ephesians 6:7

When Vanessa's friend Jessica was struggling through a divorce, Vanessa tried to be present for her friend, offering babysitting, hot meals, and a listening ear. Jessica, consumed with anxiety about her future, was not always appreciative of the sacrifices Vanessa made to support her. "It was a tough year," Vanessa remembers now. "Our friendship has regained its balance, but there were times I prayed for guidance because I felt Jessica was taking my efforts for granted." Dear God, my efforts to uplift others are not always reciprocated—or even appreciated. May I do the right thing for you, not for gratitude or anything I might receive in return.

And he said unto them, Take heed, and beware of covetousness: for a man's life consisteth not in the abundance of the things which he possesseth.

Luke 12:15

Father, you've shown me that coveting isn't always as straightforward as wishing I had someone else's house or car. The covetous corruption that creeps in can wear any number of disguises, such as begrudging the fact that someone has been blessed in some way that I haven't. It can be despising someone else's success or hoping for their failure so I won't feel left behind. The list goes on, but the essence is my discontent with my own lot in life as I compare myself with someone else. Set me free today to enjoy the blessings you've provided without spoiling them with pointless comparisons.

My God, I thank you for the blessings of the single life. One of your plans was for people to get married and have children. But I know that your good and perfect will is also for some of us to live unmarried and not have children. For this life I thank you. For the gift to be free to learn to love without clinging. To seek relationships without owning, to offer my love and kindness among many friends.

Yes, Lord, at times I am lonely, like all people can be. So I ask you to fill those times of emptiness with your presence. Enter into the barren places with your refreshing water of life. And as I continue on this path—living by myself—keep my friends and family close, no matter how far away they live. Give me peace in my daily work, joy in the pursuit of wholeness, and comfort in the solitary nights. And please continue to give me a giving heart. For I know, Lord, I am blessed.

JANUARY 21

And Mizpah; for he said, The Lord watch between me and thee, when we are absent one from another.

Genesis 31:49

O Lord, how hard it is to say goodbye to loved ones visiting from thousands of miles away. Help us be mindful that even on days when we can't see their smiles or feel their hugs, you are lovingly watching over all of us. We are connected in a special way through you, Lord. Spiritually, we are never far apart.

JANUARY 22

*He loveth righteousness and judgment:
the earth is full of the goodness
of the Lord.*

Psalm 33:5

God, your love is evident all around us. If we were detectives looking for clues about your love, we'd be able to gather lots of evidence in a short time just by contemplating this world you have made. Taking a moment each day to marvel at your works is not only an affirmation of the reality of your love, but also a meaningful act of worship as we delight in you—the one who has so plainly inscribed your love everywhere.

All scripture is given by inspiration of God, and is profitable for doctrine, for reproof, for correction, for instruction in righteousness.

2 Timothy 3:16

Your Word really does cut to the heart of the matter when it comes to what life is about, Lord. It doesn't let me hide behind excuses, pretenses, or lies. It gives me the straight scoop without any meaningless frills. That kind of honesty is hard to find in this world—especially accompanied by the absolute love that fuels it. As you lay open my heart with your truth, help me not to run and hide; help me to trust your love enough to allow you to complete the "surgery" that will bring the health and well-being my soul longs for.

JANUARY 24

O give thanks unto the Lord; for he is good: for his mercy endureth for ever.

Psalm 136:1

My son Tyler is three, and he can be sweet one moment, then overcome by storms of temper the next. The other day, he was tired and had a meltdown when I asked him to put away his toys before dinner. As a parent, I am not always as even-tempered as I should be. But this was one of those times when I had the patience to do it right. I drew Tyler onto my lap and rocked him until he calmed down. As my son and I sat together, looking out at the quiet evening street, I thought of God's patience when I rail against the storms of life. Lord, I am grateful to you because you are always good and merciful to me.

I awoke at dawn one morning
From a restless night of sorrow,
Praying that with the daylight
Might come a bright tomorrow.
My heart as cold and hopeless
As winter's deepest chill,
I cried out for understanding
And to know my Father's will.
While treading up a garden path
Hushed in the fragrant air;
I spied a tender rose,
Its petals bowed as if in prayer.
As I gazed in silent awe,
It occurred to me—He knows!
The tears my Lord has shed for me
Are the dew upon the rose.

I know that thou canst do every thing,
and that no thought can be
withholden from thee.

Job 42:2

I've heard it said, "You're only as sick as your secrets." God, give me the courage to present all of myself to you, all of the time, the good and the bad. Although you can read me like a book, I feel shame when I keep things from you. Help me to open myself up. Thank you, God.

That if thou shalt confess with thy mouth the Lord Jesus, and shalt believe in thine heart that God hath raised him from the dead, thou shalt be saved.

Romans 10:9

Brooke's friend Amanda, an agnostic, has always been comfortable expressing her ideas about religion. Though their viewpoints differ, Brooke has always respected Amanda's ability to speak calmly and clearly about her perspective. And engaging in dialogue with her friend has helped Brooke, who draws strength from her faith, to articulate her own ideas. "It's funny, but I learned, from Amanda, to be unafraid of expressing what I believe," she said. "Having to explain my faith has even strengthened it." God, may I never be embarrassed by my faith or feel shy about explaining what I believe. Speaking my belief strengthens that belief.

For the Lord is good; his mercy is everlasting; and his truth endureth to all generations.

Psalm 100:5

Lord, if I were to boil down all the good news in the universe and look to see what I'd ended up with, there would be the eternal realities of your goodness, your love, and your faithfulness. And in this world, I don't have to look far for them—family, food, shelter, clothing, seasons, tides, sun, moon, stars, life, beauty, truth, salvation. And that's just a sampling, a preview of a much longer list. I'm moved to praise you and to tell you how much I love you back.

Dear Lord, I am blessed to have such good friends in my life, friends who share my sadness and my joy, my pain and my excitement, and who are always there for me when I need them. Just as I can lean on you for anything, Lord, I know you have given me these angels on Earth whom I can lean on as well. The love of these wonderful people fills my soul. I could not imagine living without them. May I always do for them what they have done for me.

Friendship is one of the sweetest joys of life. Many might have failed beneath the bitterness of their trial had they not found a friend.

—Charles Spurgeon

Better is the end of a thing than the beginning thereof: and the patient in spirit is better than the proud in spirit.

Ecclesiastes 7:8

We become discouraged when we try to live according to our own time clocks. We want what we want, and we want it this very minute. Then, when we don't get it, we sink in the quicksand of hopelessness and defeat. Only when we realize that God is at work in our lives will we begin to relax and let things happen in due season. Fruit will not ripen any faster because we demand it but will ripen in all its sweet splendor when it is ready in spite of our demands.

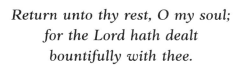

Return unto thy rest, O my soul;
for the Lord hath dealt
bountifully with thee.

Psalm 116:7

O God of rest and rejuvenation, guide me to
find ways to let your nurturing reach me. I
need to be healthy and well-rested in order
to provide, lead, and inspire. Burning the
candle at both ends all the time is hardly
an example I'm proud of.

FEBRUARY

Please let me help you
However I can.
Long ages ago
It was God's plan
For me to serve,
To love and to share—
Helping ease another's
Burden of care.
So let me be
God's loving gift to you
Because in serving others,
I am blessed, too.

*Let me find favour in thy sight, my
lord; for that thou hast comforted me.*

Ruth 2:13

Holy One, I have striven to do what is right
in your eyes. I have followed your Word
and obeyed your laws to the best of my
ability. I now ask that you will be with me
and comfort me. My needs are great and
my power is small, but in you all things are
possible. Please remove my burdens from me,
for they are too heavy to carry without your
help. Soothe me, love me, and care for me.
I ask as your child, Amen.

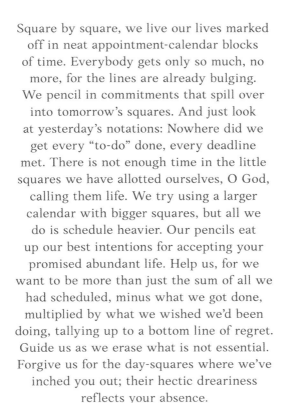

Square by square, we live our lives marked
off in neat appointment-calendar blocks
of time. Everybody gets only so much, no
more, for the lines are already bulging.
We pencil in commitments that spill over
into tomorrow's squares. And just look
at yesterday's notations: Nowhere did we
get every "to-do" done, every deadline
met. There is not enough time in the little
squares we have allotted ourselves, O God,
calling them life. We try using a larger
calendar with bigger squares, but all we
do is schedule heavier. Our pencils eat
up our best intentions for accepting your
promised abundant life. Help us, for we
want to be more than just the sum of all we
had scheduled, minus what we got done,
multiplied by what we wished we'd been
doing, tallying up to a bottom line of regret.
Guide us as we erase what is not essential.
Forgive us for the day-squares where we've
inched you out; their hectic dreariness
reflects your absence.

And not only so, but we glory in tribulations also: knowing that tribulation worketh patience; And patience, experience; and experience, hope: And hope maketh not ashamed; because the love of God is shed abroad in our hearts by the Holy Ghost which is given unto us.

Romans 5:3–5

There is every reason to give up and give in, steadfast God, for days are a struggling drudgery. When I falter, remind me that with you I am as resilient as crocuses blooming in the snow.

FEBRUARY 5

There is much to drag us back, O Lord:
empty pursuits, trivial pleasures, unworthy
cares. There is much to frighten us away:
pride that makes us reluctant to accept
help; cowardice that recoils from sharing
your suffering; anguish at the prospect
of confessing our sins to you. But you are
stronger than all these forces. We call you
our redeemer and saviour because you
redeem us from our empty, trivial existence,
you save us from our foolish fears. This is
your work, which you have completed and
will continue to complete every moment.

—Søren Kierkegaard

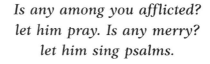

*Is any among you afflicted?
let him pray. Is any merry?
let him sing psalms.*

James 5:13

Angie's mother Gwen always tried to include God in her daily life. When Gwen faced challenges, she prayed. When she experienced joy, she sang hymns. Now that Angie is a mother herself, she tries to model this same way of being. "By speaking up and reaching out to God in good times as well as bad, I feel more connected spiritually," Angie says. "My mom gave me that gift, and I hope to pass it on to my son." Dear God, connecting with you is a form of speaking up; may I always remember this!

God of providence, as I work to satisfy the hunger and thirst of my spouse and children, I can feel your presence here in my kitchen, directing me and loving me. I remember with a thankful heart that you feed my family, too. I may appease their physical hunger, but you satisfy their hungry hearts with heavenly food—"the Bread of Life"— your son, Jesus Christ.

O Lord, who each day gives us our daily bread, bless my kitchen today as I use it to prepare nourishment for my family. My heart overflows as I joyfully cook and serve the meals in an act of love and worship.

Watch, dear Lord, with those who wake,
Or watch, or weep tonight,
And give your angels charge
Over those who sleep.
Tend your sick ones, O Lord Christ,
Rest your weary ones.
Bless your dying ones.
Soothe your suffering ones.
Pity your afflicted ones.
Shield your joyous ones.
And all for your love's sake.
Amen.
—St. Augustine

And the Lord God said, It is not good that the man should be alone; I will make him an help meet for him.

Genesis 2:18

My wife and I have been married for 25 years. Around the time we celebrated that milestone anniversary, we each began to pursue self-employment ventures that allow us to work from home. Several friends have laughingly asked if we get on one another's nerves, but working from home has actually been a real joy for us both. We like working together in the living room with music playing in the background. We both love the company of our cats. I really enjoy that my wife and I can eat lunch together, and sometimes we'll take a break in the afternoon and swim laps at the Y. My wife is my best friend. God, thank you for the everyday companionship that a strong marriage brings.

FEBRUARY 10

I remember hearing someone say once,
"If God seems far away, guess who moved?"
It's true, Lord: Sometimes I drift far away
from you. I neglect reading your Word, I
let my prayer life go by the wayside, and I
get all tangled up in my attempts to handle
everything on my own. I usually come to a
sudden realization of how much I need you,
and I am grateful for the epiphany!
Even though I'm the one who's moved so far
away, you don't hold it against me;
you simply call me back.

That is, that I may be comforted together with you by the mutual faith both of you and me.

Romans 1:12

Sharon has been participating in a morning exercise class for three years; the class gets her day off to a good start. A few weeks ago she was surprised when a classmate, a woman she hardly knows, approached her after the morning session and thanked her for always maintaining an attitude of positivity. "She said my cheerfulness uplifts her," Sharon remembers. "I was gratified— and humbled to realize that how I act can affect even those I barely know." You never know whom you might inspire through your actions. Dear God, may I live a life of faith, cheer, and humility; help me to live in a way that uplifts others.

For thy mercy is great above the heavens: and thy truth reacheth unto the clouds.

Psalm 108:4

His love is wider than our worries, longer than our loneliness, stronger than our sorrows, deeper than our doubts, and higher than our hostilities. This is why valleys are so wide, rivers so long, winds so strong, oceans so deep, and the sky is so high— with these, we can have a picture of the wonder of his love.

Bless them which persecute you:
bless, and curse not.

Romans 12:14

Lord, the last thing I want to say to the person who tailgates me in traffic is "Bless you." And I certainly don't want to pray for them to have a good day. Oh, but how graciously you've blessed my life, even though I've acted like a jerk on countless occasions. So please help me to peel my focus off of how I'm being treated and redirect it toward how I've been treated by you. Then I'll be able to draw from your great reservoir of mercy and pay it forward in the form of a blessing instead of a curse.

FEBRUARY 14

On Valentine's Day, a day to say "I love you," we remember you, O God. We are able to love only because you first loved us. You taught us how to love you and each other— our family and our neighbors.

We want our children to know your perfect love, and we invite the fragrance of your love to permeate our home.

Heavenly Father, you are the author of love. Write your name on our children's hearts, so they may enjoy the wondrous gifts you have prepared for those who love you.

God will never leave thee,

All thy wants He knows,

Feels the pains that grieve thee,

Sees thy cares and woes.

Raise thine eyes to heaven

When thy spirits quail,

When, by tempests driven,

Heart and courage fail.

When in grief we languish,

He will dry the tear,

Who His children's anguish

Soothes with succour near.

All our woe and sadness,

In this world below,

Balance not the gladness,

We in heaven shall know.

—General Hymn #286,
Book of Common Prayer

FEBRUARY 16

The words of wise men are heard in quiet more than the cry of him that ruleth among fools.

Ecclesiastes 9:17

The world is a noisy place. From family to office to leisure and routes in between, the air vibrates with ear-grabbing, relentless chatter. I yearn for quiet conversations with the God of still, small voices. My spirit, like my body, is easily bruised by too much noise. Help me, O God, hear you. Help me shut out the world when you talk.

Father in heaven, sometimes I feel anger welling up inside me, and I need to turn to you for counsel. Please stay near to me and help me to find ways to express my emotions without harming another's feelings or getting myself so upset I cannot see past my own feelings. I need to understand myself, express myself, and accept myself—all within the bounds of your teachings.
Amen.

And Jesus said unto them, I am the bread of life: he that cometh to me shall never hunger; and he that believeth on me shall never thirst.

John 6:35

You truly do satisfy my spiritual hunger, Lord! In fact, when I'm away from you due to distractions or detours of my own making, I deeply feel the lack of you in my life. But then when I stop and take time to "feed" on your Word and spend time "drinking in" your comfort, I am strengthened and refreshed again. How true your Word is!

Someone may ask, "What's the difference between humility and humiliation?" A simple way to look at it is that humility is voluntary and peaceful, while humiliation is compulsory and painful. Practically speaking, it's better for me to think rightly about myself in relation to God and others (i.e., to walk in humility) than to think I'm "all that" and experience the humiliation of an extreme reality check. As I walk in true humility, there's the added bonus that God will send honor my way—and the honor he will set up for me will be sweeter than any I could try to grab for myself.

Lord, speak to me through these pages.

Let me hear your gentle words

Come whispering through the ages

And thundering through the world.

Challenge me and change me,

Comfort me and calm me.

Completely rearrange me,

Soothe me with a psalm.

Teach me how to please you,

Show me how to live.

Inspire me to praise you

For all the love you give.

Creator of all, I hold up to you our aging
pet. She's still enjoying life, but she's
slowing down, and we know we will face
some difficult decisions soon. Please let us
appreciate the time we have,
and not prolong any pain.

FEBRUARY 22

*And when thou art spoiled, what wilt
thou do? Though thou clothest thyself
with crimson, though thou deckest thee
with ornaments of gold, though thou
rentest thy face with painting,
in vain shalt thou make thyself fair;
thy lovers will despise thee,
they will seek thy life.*

Jeremiah 4:30

Lord, how much time do we spend looking
into a mirror, and how often do we see you
there? We were made in your image, but
rather than focusing on that, we often focus
on all the things we'd like to change. When
others look at us, do they see our meager
attempts to make our lips fuller and our
eyelashes longer, or do they see the light of
your love shining through our eyes? Teach
us to focus less on our own appearance
and concentrate more on presenting your
face to those around us. It is you the
world needs, not us.

Love is others oriented. Jesus' example has shown us what true love is like: "Hereby perceive we the love of God, because he laid down his life for us: and we ought to lay down our lives for the brethren" (1 John 3:16). Each time you set aside your druthers to see to someone else's best interest, you're exercising that others-oriented kind of love that Jesus demonstrated. And since your motivation for self-sacrifice is out of kindness and compassion (rather than compulsion or any form of fear), the joy in giving makes each personal sacrifice well worthwhile.

*Thy word is a lamp unto my feet,
and a light unto my path.*

Psalm 119:105

As a college student living in the United States, I have many advantages, and it's easy to fall into the trap of feeling that, given all I have going for me, I should "be the best at everything." I am hard on myself when I don't get the best grade, for example, or when I perceive that I'm not as physically fit as some of my dorm mates. God, help me to remember that there is always room for improvement, a condition I share with everyone else on Earth, and that your Word can comfort me, guide me, and serve as the ultimate "self-improvement manual."

Then spake the Lord to Paul in the night by a vision, Be not afraid, but speak, and hold not thy peace.

Acts 18:9

When sixteen-year-old Kate auditioned for the school play, she was surprised to be cast in a substantial role. She loved rehearsals and connected with fellow cast members, but as the date of the show approached, she found herself increasingly consumed with doubt. What if she froze on stage? She wished she could drop out of the play, but her dad encouraged her to pray for courage. She did so. "I'm so glad I stuck with it," Kate says now. God, I know it's okay to have stage fright, but I mustn't let fear stop me. Thank you for helping me work through my fears.

The mighty God, even the Lord, hath spoken, and called the earth from the rising of the sun unto the going down thereof.

Psalm 50:1

Slowly but surely, the days are getting longer again. I'm impatient for spring to arrive. But before it does...I thank you for the blessings of the winter, God. The holidays, the snow days, the celebration of your birth. I thank you for warm clothes and hot chocolate, and the days the car started despite the chill. I thank you even for bare tree branches and gray slush!

And as the days get longer, let me appreciate the extra sunlight as a gift, a daily grace that reminds me of your love.

FEBRUARY 27

Lord, sometimes I long to stand out. I notice
others with shinier hair, amazing figures,
and impeccable outfits, and I feel so plain.
At these times, help me to remember that I
should be at work cultivating the gentle and
quiet spirit that is precious to you. This type
of spirit may not call out, "Here I am!" but
over the long run, it accomplishes much. I
am doing what I can, and I leave the rest to
you. I trust that you will bring all to fruition.

And he arose, and came to his father. But when he was yet a great way off, his father saw him, and had compassion, and ran, and fell on his neck, and kissed him. And the son said unto him, Father, I have sinned against heaven, and in thy sight, and am no more worthy to be called thy son.

Luke 15:20–21

I love the story of the prodigal son. It reminds me of the bond mothers and children share, and it reminds me of the simple fact that our children are human. They are going to make mistakes; sometimes they are going to disappoint us, deeply. But as mothers, we are called upon to love our children, and forgive them, even when they have hurt us. (God, I suppose you know exactly what I mean: Even when I make mistakes, your love for me remains a constant.) Dear God, may I have the strength and wisdom to always love my children and be there for them, even when they disobey.

FEBRUARY 29

Lord, if only all the false gods that lure us were clearly labeled. We are introduced to worldly ambition, wealth, physical perfection, romance—any number of attractive enticements—and it isn't until we realize that the pursuit of them is using up way too much of our resources that we discover we have made these things our gods. Forgive us, Lord. Help us to keep even good things in balance and never to pursue anything with more fervor than we pursue our relationship with you.

MARCH

MARCH 1

And Jesus being full of the Holy Ghost returned from Jordan, and was led by the Spirit into the wilderness.

Luke 4:1

Thank you, God, for this new month. This month brings the first inklings of spring to my area, though the trees are still bare. But that seems appropriate, during this month that takes place during the season of Lent. Lord, this month, empty my heart of distractions. Walk with me to the desert and stay with me there, as you pare away those things that draw me away from you.

Strengthen ye the weak hands, and confirm the feeble knees.

Isaiah 35:3

Little things can mean a lot. Emma's mom Diane had had a hard day at work: Emma saw it on her mom's face the moment Diane came through the door. Without prompting, Emma made dinner; she even threw together an impromptu dessert, cooked in a mug in the microwave and, crucially, involving chocolate. "I was so discouraged when I got home," Diane remembers. "But my evening was, truly, transformed by loving-kindness." Lord, you want us to uplift the weak and exhausted. May I provide support to those who are worn down in life.

MARCH 3

Some prayers are best left unfinished,
God of abundance, and this will be an
ongoing conversation between us. Each
day I discover new gifts you offer me, and
the list of reasons to be thankful grows.
As I accept your gifts and live with them
thankfully, guide me to become a person
who shares with others so that they, too, can
live abundantly. May someone, somewhere,
someday say of me, "I am thankful to have
this person in my life."

MARCH 4

But speaking the truth in love, may grow up into him in all things, which is the head, even Christ.

Ephesians 4:15

Selma's sister Heather had always enjoyed a glass or two of wine over dinner, but increasingly, Selma noticed that Heather was drinking in excess. Selma doesn't like confrontation, but things came to a head after an unpleasant, alcohol-fueled incident at a family dinner. With love and some trepidation, Selma sat down with Heather and encouraged her to seek treatment. It was a difficult, but necessary, conversation. Though tears were shed, Heather agreed to get help. Dear Lord, speaking the truth publicly is not always easy to do, but it is important. It is an act of love. Please help me to do so with strength and grace.

MARCH 5

Thus saith the Lord, The people which were left of the sword found grace in the wilderness; even Israel, when I went to cause him to rest. The Lord hath appeared of old unto me, saying, Yea, I have loved thee with an everlasting love: therefore with lovingkindness have I drawn thee.

Jeremiah 31:2–3

Lord, as we move through this Lenten season, let me not be afraid of the wilderness. Let me not be afraid of unanswered questions, of uncertain paths, of scarcity. Let me trust in you and your loving-kindness, that I will have what I need when I need it. Let me trust in your "daily bread," and not get wound up in worries about the future.

The Lord shall fight for you,
and ye shall hold your peace.

Exodus 14:14

Life's not fair, and I stomp my foot in
frustration. The powerful get more so as
the rest of us shrink, dreams for peace are
shattered as bullies get the upper hand, and
despair is a tempting pit to fall into. Help
me hold on, for you are a God of justice and
dreams, of turning life upside down. Let me
help; thanks for listening in the meantime.

Prioritizing spiritual realities over temporal ones is not always easy. The physical realities are tangible. I can hold a stack of bills in my hand and know that if I don't pay them, problems will arise. But those spiritual realities . . . well, the benefits (and consequences) are not always so easy to recognize or see in the moment. This is a faith issue, pure and simple. First, I need to stay calm about issues of provision. Second, I need to keep drawing near to you. Third, I need to reach out to others with your love. And after all of these things are done, I need to trust you with the results.

MARCH 8

*David was afraid of the Lord that day,
and said, How shall the ark of the
Lord come to me?*

2 Samuel 6:9

God, I made a mess of things today. I meant
well: I leapt out of bed with a smile. But as
the day progressed, I found myself losing
equanimity. It was a long commute, and
when someone cut me off I felt my temper
rising. I had to change a lunch appointment;
my friend expressed disappointment and at
that point in the day, knee-deep in work,
I felt too stressed to listen and respond
with grace. A meeting ran late; I was late
picking up my son at basketball practice and
felt guilty and anxious. I snapped at him;
I snapped at my husband. Where was the
calm, gracious person I was determined to
be only this morning? And yet through it all,
I know you love me. Thank you for always
blessing me with your loving-kindness.
Thank you for reminding me that, with you,
there is always another chance to be our
best selves.

MARCH 9

Therefore, my beloved brethren,
be ye stedfast, unmoveable, always
abounding in the work of the Lord,
forasmuch as ye know that your
labour is not in vain in the Lord.

1 Corinthians 15:58

We can take a lesson from the precious water lily. For no matter what outside force or pressure is put upon the lily, it always rises back to the water's surface again to feel the nurturing sunlight upon its leaves and petals. We must be like the lily, steadfast and true in the face of every difficulty, that we too may rise above our problems and feel God's light upon our faces again.

MARCH 10

Train up a child in the way he should go: and when he is old, he will not depart from it.

Proverbs 22:6

Lord, I tried to teach my children the way to go. Sometimes I didn't get it right. Now it is up to you. May your Spirit bring to their minds those things they learned about you and your Word. May these truths guide them as they make their own choices and build their own relationships. Help me to rest in your promise, even when I can't see it happening. Yet.

MARCH 11

But I would strengthen you with my mouth, and the moving of my lips should asswage your grief.

Job 16:5

One of my oldest friends, Beth, recently and unexpectedly lost her husband. Dan was killed in a freak car accident, and Beth and her children have been blindsided by the loss. I have spent a lot of time with the family since the accident, and see how even the most well-meaning people have sometimes said hurtful things to Beth in their efforts to show concern. I want to avoid causing my friend any more pain, and so for the most part have tried to provide solace with my quiet presence. But I know that the right words can assuage grief. Dear Lord, grant me the wisdom to comfort my friends in their time of need. Help me to know what to say.

MARCH 12

O gracious and holy Father,

Give us wisdom to perceive you,

Intelligence to understand you,

Diligence to seek you,

Patience to wait for you,

Eyes to see you,

A heart to meditate on you,

And a life to proclaim you,

Through the power of the spirit of

Jesus Christ our Lord.

—St. Benedict

MARCH 13

They helped every one his neighbour;
and every one said to his brother,
Be of good courage.

Isaiah 41:6

Father, I thank you for the healing power
of friends and for the positive emotions
friendship brings. Thank you for sending
companions to me so we can support and
encourage one another and share our joys
and sorrows. My friends represent for me
your presence and friendship here on Earth.
Please keep them in your care, Father. We
need each other, and we need you. Amen.

MARCH 14

And Judas and Silas, being prophets also themselves, exhorted the brethren with many words, and confirmed them.

Acts 15:32

Margie has lived long, and seen much; life has not always been kind to her. But experience has made Margie wise, not bitter, and she has the gift of imparting that wisdom in a gentle, offhand way. "I learned from her and I didn't even know I was learning!" Margie's granddaughter Alice says, adding, "This was especially important when I was a teen, and didn't think anyone had anything to teach me! Grandma's lessons are delivered with tremendous grace." Lord, teaching others can uplift! Help me to share with others what I know; help me to be a strong, wise teacher.

So God created man in his own image,
in the image of God created he him;
male and female created he them.

Genesis 1:27

"I'm fat," Lauren's 13-year-old daughter Rachel announced unhappily at breakfast one morning. "Kelly at school said so." Lauren finished preparing their eggs, then sat down with her daughter. "You are not fat," she said. "And Kelly sounds like an unhappy person." As Rachel finished her breakfast and started to gather her school things, Lauren gave her a hug. "God created you in his image, which is a pretty amazing thing," she said. "Don't ever forget you are beautiful." Dear God, on days when I am low, help me to accept myself. May I always remember that you made me in your own image!

MARCH 16

*I write unto you, little children,
because your sins are forgiven you
for his name's sake.*

1 John 2:12

Lord, sometimes I resist your grace. It's not
that I don't want to be closer to you, but I
know I don't deserve it. I stew over my past
sins, wallowing in guilt. I don't want to take
your forgiveness for granted, but neither do I
want to forget that you are always reaching
out to me, ready to draw me back to you.

MARCH 17

And he said, Of a truth I say unto you, that this poor widow hath cast in more than they all: For all these have of their abundance cast in unto the offerings of God: but she of her penury hath cast in all the living that she had.

Luke 21:3–4

I ask you for a spirit of both generosity and trust. Generosity prompts us to want to share what we have with others, to take care of our neighbors. Trust lets us believe that you will take care of us and provide our daily bread. When I am blessed with abundance, let me give with abundance. And when I feel scarcity, let me give anyway.

God, I couldn't help noticing all the
loveliness you placed in the world today!
This morning I witnessed a sunrise that
made my heart beat faster. Later I watched
a father gently help his child across a busy
parking lot; his tenderness was much like
yours. While inside a department store, I
spied an elderly couple sitting on a bench.
I could hear the man cracking jokes; their
laughter lifted my spirits. Then early this
evening, I walked by a woman tending her
flower bed; she took great pleasure in her
work, and her garden was breathtaking.
Later, I talked with a friend who is helping
some needy families; her genuine compassion
inspired me. Thank you, Lord, for everything
that is beautiful and good in the world.

MARCH 19

Being confident of this very thing, that he which hath begun a good work in you will perform it until the day of Jesus Christ.

Philippians 1:6

God, help me become a powerful loving presence in the world. Set before me directions to the path meant for me, a path that allows me to fully express your will through my words, deeds, and actions. Amen.

MARCH 20

Then shall we know, if we follow on to know the Lord: his going forth is prepared as the morning; and he shall come unto us as the rain, as the latter and former rain unto the earth.

Hosea 6:3

How certain the seasons are, Lord! How faithfully you usher them in one after the other, each in its assigned order. The spring has come with its rains once again, just as I knew it would. And spring's arrival reminds me that you—the faithful creator—have promised to dwell with those who long to know you, those who search for you and look for your return.

MARCH 21

Lord, your love gives me all the strength I need to accomplish anything. Knowing that you deem me worthy of your love is the foundation of my entire faith. Understanding that you won't ever stop loving me is my shelter from the storms of life that challenge my peace and serenity. I know that I am always going to be loved no matter what I do, even when I don't always do the right thing. And that knowing fuels the desire to try to do the right thing, even when it is the harder thing to do. You have deemed me worthy. Now let me live up to that worthiness. Amen.

MARCH 22

Lord, I have passed another day
And come to thank thee for thy care.
Forgive my faults in work or play
And listen to my evening prayer.
Thy favor gives me daily bread
And friends, who all my wants supply:
And safely now I rest my head,
Preserved and guarded by Thine eye.
Amen.
—Traditional evening prayer

MARCH 23

*Behold, the former things are come
to pass, and new things do I declare:
before they spring forth
I tell you of them.*

Isaiah 42:9

Enliven my imagination, God of new life, so
that I can see through today's troubles to
coming newness. Surround me with your
caring so that I can live as if the new has
already begun.

MARCH 24

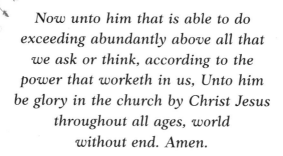

*Now unto him that is able to do
exceeding abundantly above all that
we ask or think, according to the
power that worketh in us, Unto him
be glory in the church by Christ Jesus
throughout all ages, world
without end. Amen.*

Ephesians 3:20–22

Father, sometimes I see people who seem to
have found work perfectly suited to them,
and I wonder if I am fulfilling my purpose.
Thank you for reminding me that you are at
work in me, bringing about your purposes,
which are not always clear to me. You take
even small gifts—as you did with the loaves
and the fishes—and you make them multiply.

Human beings are the only creatures that strive to be something they are not. Perhaps we should take a lesson from the birds of the sky, who never ache to be anything other than creatures able to fly at will upon a lifting breeze. Or we should learn from the fish of the sea, who don't doubt their own ability to glide through blue waters dappled with sunlight. Or maybe we should spend some time watching wild horses thunder over the open plains, and we would see that not once do they stop to wish they were anything more than what God made them: glorious, beautiful, and free.

MARCH 26

Be still, and know that I am God.

Psalm 46:10

Easter is coming soon. Part of me wants to
skip ahead to the joy of that season,
as I plan for the family gathering and
shop for an outfit.

But we are not quite there, yet, so let me
rest in stillness with you for a while yet.
Let me take time to reflect each day, even
if those reflections on repentance are not
always comfortable.

For the law was given by Moses, but grace and truth came by Jesus Christ.

John 1:17

Christ is no Moses, no exactor, no giver of laws, but a giver of grace, a Savior; he is infinite mercy and goodness, freely and bountifully giving to us.

—Martin Luther

MARCH 28

Give, and it shall be given unto you;
good measure, pressed down, and
shaken together, and running over,
shall men give into your bosom.
For with the same measure that
ye mete withal it shall be
measured to you again.

Luke 6:38

A kind act by a stranger is a wonderful
surprise! I don't expect someone to let me
go ahead in line at the store or to return an
item I had lost. What a blessing it is when
people reach out to others. Thank you for
the small acts that make my day better,
and thank you for the opportunity to be a
blessing to others by finding small ways to
make their day brighter.

Repent ye therefore, and be converted,
that your sins may be blotted out,
when the times of refreshing shall
come from the presence of the Lord.

Acts 3:19

O Lord, if you don't remember our sins,
why do we so often beat ourselves up over
them? The only possible benefit I can see
is that this way, there's less chance that
we'll repeat them. But if it be your will,
Lord—and to our benefit—grant us your
sweet forgetfulness. We accept your gift of
forgiveness, Lord. May we learn to accept
your gift of forgetfulness as well.

*I am the good shepherd, and know my
sheep, and am known of mine.*

John 10:14

Your Word says—and I've heard it
elsewhere—that a flock of sheep knows its
own shepherd's voice and won't respond to
the voice of a different shepherd. It's true of
my relationship with you, too, Lord. I know
your voice. I know when you're speaking to
my heart, and I know when I'm being coaxed
by "other voices"—wrong desires, worldly
values, anxiety, pride, and the like. Thanks
for helping me see the difference.
Coax me to follow the sound of
your voice today and always.

Lord, I'm looking forward to this new phase of my life. It is full of promise and hope, though I know that challenges will surely come as well. I know you have all the courage, strength, faithfulness, and love I need to meet each moment from a perspective of peace. I just need to stay tethered to you in prayer, listening for your Spirit to guide me and turn my thoughts continually back toward you. That's the key to a good life.

APRIL

APRIL 1

It is like a grain of mustard seed, which a man took, and cast into his garden; and it grew, and waxed a great tree; and the fowls of the air lodged in the branches of it.

Luke 13:19

Just a tiny seed of faith, watered with love, wisdom, and hard work, grows into a majestic tree of blessings.

Spring is the season of moving—the real estate market picks up, and "for sale" signs crop up in the neighborhood. Please bless all who are preparing for moves, that they find a house that can be a true home. Please bless those who are not moving by choice—those who are relocating for a spouse's job, or no longer able to maintain their home because of age. Please help us all remember that you go with us everywhere, and that we do not need to fear change when you are with us.

APRIL 3

*From the end of the earth will I
cry unto thee, when my heart is
overwhelmed: lead me to the rock that
is higher than I. For thou hast been
a shelter for me, and a strong tower
from the enemy.*

Psalm 61:2–3

Lord, how we want to run to you in times
of need—and how blessed we are that we
always find you available. You always take us
in and calm our weary spirits. You, O Lord,
are mighty and unchangeable! At times when
everything seems shaky and uncertain,
you are firm and immovable.
We praise you, Lord!

APRIL 4

Lord Jesus, you are medicine to me when I
am sick, strength to me when I need help,
life itself when I fear death, the way when
I long for heaven, the light when all is dark,
and food when I need nourishment.
Glory be to you forever. Amen.

—St. Ambrose

APRIL 5

The next day John seeth Jesus coming unto him, and saith, Behold the Lamb of God, which taketh away the sin of the world.

John 1:29

Lord, the world just wasn't ready for your appearance by the Jordan. There you were, the king they so desired, yet they didn't know you. Let us welcome you into our world today as wholeheartedly as John the Baptist did when you appeared in the flesh! For you came to be our hope and our salvation. Humbly you came, but mightily you saved.

APRIL 6

As every man hath received the gift, even so minister the same one to another, as good stewards of the manifold grace of God.

1 Peter 4:10

One of my friends is going through a difficult time, and I don't know what to do. I feel so helpless. You know his needs, Lord, better than I do. I hold him up to you in prayer. If there is some way you can use me to help him, I ask that you plant the idea in my head. I ask that any words I say to him be inspired by you.

APRIL 7

Trust in the Lord with all thine heart; and lean not unto thine own understanding.

Proverbs 3:5

Sometimes I work so hard to control everything that I need to be reminded to have faith and "let go." Last night my head was in a whirl: I lay in bed and stared into the darkness, worrying about bills, my workload, and if my husband and I would have time to care for the yard. My mind churned as I envisioned schemes, schedules, emails I might write, and ways to exert control. It was only when I "let go" and decided to give my concerns over to you that I gained some measure of peace, and was able to sleep. Lord, thank you for your support and guidance as I navigate my busy days. May I have the faith to trust you over my own understanding.

APRIL 8

Confess your faults one to another, and pray one for another, that ye may be healed. The effectual fervent prayer of a righteous man availeth much.

James 5:16

Who shall I pray for today, Lord? I don't want to pray only for my needs and my wants, but to hold others up to you in prayer. Please bring to my mind the names of those who most need prayer today.

APRIL 9

For bodily exercise profiteth little: but godliness is profitable unto all things, having promise of the life that now is, and of that which is to come.

1 Timothy 4:8

We live in a society that is so focused on the physical body. We run, walk, exercise, and go to the gym, comparing our bodies to others. We diet and "watch our figures." We become so obsessed with our bodies, we forget the importance of keeping our minds and spirits in shape. But God promises us an amazing life when we stay focused on his presence. He even promises us a life beyond this one. God, I pray for a strong and resilient body and a powerful spirit to serve you with. I know my own self-worth is developed as I help and serve others.

APRIL 10

Lord, I pray that my words and actions may be a comfort to those in need. Let me see the world around me through your eyes, that I might notice the small wounds and sorrows that each of us carries within us, hidden from view and known only to you. I ask that you use my hands to do your work here on Earth, to heal the hurting, to feed the hungry, to befriend the lonely. May I be an instrument of your endless love, that I might share your Spirit generously and abundantly with everyone I encounter. Amen.

APRIL 11

And Naomi said unto her daughter in law, Blessed be he of the Lord, who hath not left off his kindness to the living and to the dead. And Naomi said unto her, The man is near of kin unto us, one of our next kinsmen.

Ruth 2:20

We are all connected, Lord, and may I impress upon my children the importance of this fact. It is one thing to talk about our connection to all living things but it is quite another to live it. Help me to demonstrate, not only in my words but also my actions, the fundamental role loving-kindness should play in our lives. Whether it be aid to an injured animal, support and a listening ear to one who grieves, or respectful words spoken about someone who is deceased, may I put good into the world without expectation of recognition or reward. May I do good simply for the sake of doing good, and may I never stop showing kindness to those in need.

APRIL 12

What a day. When all else fails, rearrange
the furniture. Lend a shoulder, God of
change, as I scoot the couch to a new spot.
Like wanderers to your promised land,
I need a fresh perspective. My life has
turned topsy-turvy, and I need a new place
to sit . . . first with you, then the rest of my
world of family, friends, job. I need to be
prepared for whatever happens next, and
nothing says it like a redone room. I smile as
I take my new seat; this is a better view.

APRIL 13

O Lord, our Lord, how excellent is thy name in all the earth! who hast set thy glory above the heavens.

Psalm 8:1

This morning I am marveling at the birds at the bird feeder, Lord. Those little creatures are so fascinating! Their plumage, the variety of sizes, shapes, beaks, tails, wings, calls . . . I feel a sense of pure delight at their existence. I can find so many things to be in awe of in this great, wide universe you have made. You have made it all to speak of your majesty—to tell us what you are like. I turn my heart toward heaven today, to worship and give glory to you, Lord.

APRIL 14

But I have trusted in thy mercy; my heart shall rejoice in thy salvation. I will sing unto the Lord, because he hath dealt bountifully with me.

Psalm 13:5–6

God's mercy is his compassion for people who don't deserve it. None of us do, really. But this mercy is a reason to rejoice. This mercy is the basis of our salvation, and the theme of our song. In his mercy he has dealt bountifully with us, beyond all expectation, merit, or hope. And it is in his mercy we trust, not in any effort of our own. Despite our brokenness and failures, God extends mercy to those who believe.

APRIL 15

Living in difficult times requires us to maintain a positive, hopeful attitude about the future. Having hope is vital for our mental, physical, and spiritual health.

Lord, help me move into the future with a steadfast spirit, looking forward in faith and hope and trusting in the promises you have made to your people.

Today I make a covenant to you that I will choose hope. If I encounter disappointment, I will choose hope. If confronted with temptation, I will choose hope. In the face of fear, I will choose hope. If I sense doubt washing over me, I will choose hope. If I feel angry, I will choose hope. Instead of giving in to sadness or despair, I will choose hope.

In all things that come my way today, Lord, I am determined to choose hope. Regardless of what happened in the past, today—through you—I am strong enough to choose hope.

APRIL 16

For if they fall, the one will lift up his fellow: but woe to him that is alone when he falleth; for he hath not another to help him up.

Ecclesiastes 4:10

Lord, so many times when I've been down, time with a good friend has lifted me up again and helped me to face my circumstances with a better attitude. Sometimes that friend is my best friend— my husband—but other times it's one of my precious female friends who seems to intuitively know the precise advice I need. Thank you, Lord, for dear friends. May I be such a friend to others.

APRIL 17

*But when the fulness of the time was come, God sent forth his Son, made of a woman, made under the law,
To redeem them that were under the law, that we might receive the adoption of sons.*

Galatians 4:4–5

Father, it's as if time itself was aware of your plan to redeem humanity through your son. In this verse I'm reminded of your perfect timing—that nothing you do is by accident or happenstance. Jesus came at precisely the right time in history to carry out your wonderful purposes. I'll trust you, then, with the timing in my life. I'll stop fretting and wait patiently. You are in control, and I know you have a plan.

APRIL 18

*But thou, O Lord, art a God full
of compassion, and gracious,
long suffering, and plenteous
in mercy and truth.*

Psalm 86:15

It is easy to be judgmental. It is easy to
write another person off when they fall
short of our expectations. Even those we
love will disappoint us. Yesterday I was
short with my sister when she called to
let me know that she won't be able to
take our mother shopping this weekend.
I was counting on her help, and at first, I
wouldn't let myself hear her explanation:
Her own daughter is sick, and her husband,
my brother-in-law, has been pulling extra
shifts at work. It took effort for me to
overcome my own annoyance and listen to
what she had to say. Dear Lord, help me to
remember that compassion comes from you.
May I be inspired by the compassion you
show me every day, and may I in turn show
compassion to others.

Blessed are the peacemakers: for they shall be called the children of God.

Matthew 5:9

It seems that there's a peacemaker in every family—the mom or dad, sister or brother who tries really hard to move everyone toward a peaceful resolution when conflict arises. To seek the path of peace reflects God's own heart of reconciliation. When our children or protégés emulate us in good ways, we say joyfully, "That's my girl!" or "That's my boy!" Similarly, God is delighted to call us his children when we seek the path of peace.

APRIL 20

The God of my rock; in him will I trust: he is my shield, and the horn of my salvation, my high tower, and my refuge, my saviour; thou savest me from violence.

2 Samuel 22:3

Today I'll simply trust you, Father. I'll remember that you're not looking for résumés full of impressive credentials; rather, you seek hearts that trust in you. You want to enjoy a vibrant, meaningful relationship with me—a relationship in which I trust you fully. That's the starting point of a life lived for you.

APRIL 21

The Lord will strengthen him upon the bed of languishing: thou wilt make all his bed in his sickness.

Psalm 41:3

Lord Jesus Christ, my best physician, I come to thee in this my sickness. I pray thee to look upon me in tender mercy. Send thy guardian angel to watch over me and soon make me well. Amen.

—Traditional prayer

Fear not, little flock; for it is your Father's good pleasure to give you the kingdom.

Luke 12:32

Jesus speaks to us as a shepherd to his flock. The fear he speaks of is the fear of not having what we need. He just told a story about a rich man who built too many barns—and reminded his disciples that his Father takes care of the ravens and the lilies. We shouldn't worry about what we will eat or what we will drink because "your Father knoweth that ye have need of these things" (verse 30). It is not just the Father's knowledge, but the Father's pleasure that sustains us. This truth is so certain that Jesus next says, "Sell that ye have, and give alms" (verse 33). Don't cling to your stuff. The Father enjoys taking care of you. It is his good pleasure to provide for you.

And out of the ground the Lord God formed every beast of the field, and every fowl of the air; and brought them unto Adam to see what he would call them: and whatsoever Adam called every living creature, that was the name thereof.

Genesis 2:19

Thank you, God, for all the animals who have helped us to feel closer to you and your creation. Keep them safe, these trusted innocents who calm our lives and show us love. Help them find their way home if they are lost. Help them hear the voices of those who will care for them. Save them from every unsafe place.

APRIL 24

For which cause we faint not;
but though our outward man perish,
yet the inward man is
renewed day by day.

2 Corinthians 4:16

We are not promised here strength for every
thing, but for every day. We do not need
to carry the weight of tomorrow, because
God's mercy and compassion "are new every
morning" (Lamentations 3:23). Jesus said,
"Sufficient unto the day is the evil thereof."
Therefore, he says, "Take therefore no
thought for the morrow" (Matthew 6:34).

This is why we pray, "Give us day by day
our daily bread" (Luke 11:3), depending
always on the benevolence of God, "renewed
in the spirit of your mind" (Ephesians 4:23).
There is always sufficient evil. But there is
also sufficient grace. "Philip saith unto him,
Lord, show us the Father, and
it sufficeth us." (John 14:8).

I recently turned 50 and have started to see changes in my body. I have had to start watching cholesterol levels. I've had to work harder to stay trim. Sometimes I fear that my mind is not as sharp as it once was. I don't have as great a faculty for remembering things as I did when I was younger, so I rely more on lists to keep the day running smoothly. More and more, conversations with friends circle around to these types of health issues, and sometimes I feel fearful at the prospect of aging. And yet, God reminds us that even when our bodies and minds begin to break down, he renews our spirit. God, thank you for being with me at every age, in every chapter of my life.

APRIL 26

I will lift up mine eyes unto the hills, from whence cometh my help. My help cometh from the Lord, which made heaven and earth.

Psalm 121:1–2

Lord, you promise a helping hand in hard times. Today, I pray for all those who are in desperate need of help in order to survive: victims of earthquakes and tornadoes, the homeless, and the physically and emotionally destitute people of our world. Make yourself known to them, Lord. May they all see that their true help comes only from you! You who created them will not leave them without help, nor without hope.

Father, there are many events in our lives over which we have no control. However, we do have a choice either to endure trying times or to give up. Remind us that the secret of survival is remembering that our hope is in your fairness, goodness, and justice. When we put our trust in you who cannot fail us, we can remain faithful. Our trust and faithfulness produce the endurance that sees us through the tough times we all face in this life. Please help us to remember. Amen.

Faith is a living, daring confidence in God's grace. It is so sure and certain that a man could stake his life on it a thousand times.

—Martin Luther

*For with God nothing
shall be impossible.*

Luke 1:37

I am enduring a dark period, God.
Alzheimer's disease ravages my beloved
father, and I must assist him and my mother
while I try to raise my own three children
with strength, patience, and joy. Some nights
I lie awake, filled with fear that my little
family will not survive this next chapter—
one of many "Sandwich Generation" families
with children and parents to care for. Dear
God, help me remain faithful to the promise
that with you, nothing is impossible, even if
I can't see through it for myself.

Hear therefore, O Israel, and observe to do it; that it may be well with thee, and that ye may increase mightily, as the Lord God of thy fathers hath promised thee, in the land that floweth with milk and honey.

Deuteronomy 6:3

If you could use some milk and honey, rest in God's promises today. What are these promises? A mighty increase, certainly: His kindness is full of unexpected delight. He will give you more than your daily bread, although that's sufficient. He also promises safety and security. It will be well with you, he says, if you hear his Word and do it. This is his gracious promise.

Heavenly Father, when you made the
earth, you were satisfied with the job and
pronounced it "good." Because I am your
child, I find satisfaction in creating, too.
I give you thanks, Father, for the gift of
creativity. Help me never to discourage
but to encourage the sparks of creativity
in my children, so they can experience
the pleasure of struggle and fulfillment in
making something new. Only you can satisfy
our longing souls by filling them with
creative achievement.

MAY

I look at this month's calendar and see how many things I'm already committed to do! Dear Lord, please guide me through all my endeavors during this coming month. Please let me be a witness to your love by being loving myself, with everyone I encounter, whether strangers or family or friends or colleagues. And let me be mindful of the time I need to spend with you—that I not make myself so busy that I forget to sit in quiet prayer each day.

MAY 2

For who maketh thee to differ from another? and what hast thou that thou didst not receive? now if thou didst receive it, why dost thou glory, as if thou hadst not received it?

1 Corinthians 4:7

Stephanie's two sons are as different as night and day. Jon is quiet, thoughtful, and a quick study in math. His younger brother Mark is an ebullient artist. Stephanie, who tries to make sure that each boy is recognized within the family, also encourages them to appreciate what their sibling brings to the table. "I try to instill in them a feeling of confidence in their particular gifts," Stephanie says, "even as they recognize and celebrate another's talents." Dear God, you grant us unique gifts that make us different. May we glorify and celebrate those differences in one another!

MAY 3

My son, despise not the chastening of the Lord; neither be weary of his correction: For whom the Lord loveth he correcteth; even as a father the son in whom he delighteth.

Proverbs 3:11–12

Lord, correct me today. I know you want to curb my bad habits and improve my better ones. Sometimes you do this by letting me fail or suffer. Sometimes you do it by not giving me what I want or sitting me in a quiet place. Help me not to be weary of your work. I know you love me and want the best for me. Thank you, Lord, for your correction.

MAY 4

The Lord is not slack concerning his promise, as some men count slackness; but is longsuffering to us-ward, not willing that any should perish, but that all should come to repentance.

2 Peter 3:9

"Two steps forward, one step back." My mom, a physical therapist, sometimes says this to clients who feel discouraged about the long road to recovery. "But you'll get there," she always adds. Mom is a spiritual person, and she shared with me once that not only does she think her maxim applies to any process of self-improvement, it reminds her of God's faith in us. I was deeply struck by her observation! Self-improvement is a long haul, marked by setbacks and detours. And yet, God, you always are patient with me, and believe that I can better myself. Thank you for believing in my potential and efforts; I am bolstered by your patience and love.

MAY 5

There is no fear in love; but perfect love casteth out fear.

1 John 4:18

I cannot hold fear and love in my heart at the same time. When I am afraid, it crowds out every thought and emotion and I feel held hostage to it. That is when I need to turn to you, God, for the love that can cast out fear. Once I come back to your love, my heart begins to lighten and brighten, and my whole perspective changes. What looked impossible to deal with, God, now becomes less intimidating. What held me captive in the grip of panic now loosens its hold and I feel free again. Thank you, God, for the perfect love that fills my heart when I come to you in times of fear, worry, and concern.

MAY 6

God resisteth the proud, and giveth grace to the humble.

1 Peter 5:5

Dear Lord, it's tempting to look upon my life and feel prideful for all that I have accomplished. But everything I have has come from you, given freely to me because of your grace and not because of my actions. I go to you now in humility, reminded of my weaknesses and sins and thankful for the abundance of gifts you have given me. I am yours, pledged in your son's holy blood to obey your Word. Amen.

Then the lord of that servant was moved with compassion, and loosed him, and forgave him the debt.

Matthew 18:27

God, I aspire to be the person you want me to be, to live the life you want for me, but sometimes I struggle. I have a friend to whom I lent money; it has become apparent that not only will he not be able to repay what he owes, but he has also been avoiding me. I caught sight of him in town yesterday, and he literally crossed the street to avoid any interaction. Even when I called out to him, he would not meet my eye. I know he is ashamed that he cannot repay me, but I'm disappointed in him. I wish I'd never lent him the money. Please grant me the compassion and grace to forgive this debt, and move on.

MAY 8

And he said, Blessed be the Lord God of Israel, which spake with his mouth unto David my father, and hath with his hand fulfilled it.

1 Kings 8:15

Lord, help me to hear what you say and believe you will do it. You kept your promises to Abraham. You kept your promises to David. And you will keep your promises to me. Everything I need is always and only in your hand. So today, when I have doubts or fear or need, help me to remember your Word and wait for you to keep it. Your hand is at work, fulfilling every promise you make. Thank you.

Ye shall receive power, after that the Holy Ghost is come upon you: and ye shall be witnesses unto me both in Jerusalem, and in all Judaea, and in Samaria, and unto the uttermost part of the earth.

Acts 1:8

I call them my "blue days": when the demands of life deplete me. On these days it's hard to imagine that I can do all the things I need to do: work, cook, clean, weed the backyard, help my son with math and my daughter to untangle a thorny problem with a friend. I feel distracted and out of sorts. You feel far away. God, help me to remember that you fill your believers with power. Help me to tap into that power so I may stride into the world with energy, purpose, and joy. Thank you for your Spirit every day, especially on days when I am down.

In this was manifested the love of God toward us, because that God sent his only begotten Son into the world, that we might live through him.

1 John 4:9

Love isn't just a word; it's a verb, an action. Love falls flat when it is simply spoken, with no power behind it. God sent his son to manifest the word of his love into form and action, and we are blessed because of it. Now it is our turn to put our love into the world and spread the blessings. God, show us how we can become more loving. Show us how we can manifest miracles for each other, beyond just saying we believe in them. Show us how we can be love itself. Love isn't just a word. It is you, God, in action.

*Lo, children are an heritage of the
Lord: and the fruit of the womb
is his reward.*

Psalm 127:3

Father, you have enriched my life with many
identities—daughter, student, wife, and
mother. Richness and joy have followed me
through each phase of my life, and I have
wholeheartedly accepted and enjoyed each
role. But you knew, didn't you, Lord, that
the title of mother would make such a strong
claim on my heart? How I praise you for the
greatest of your gifts, my children, and for
the fulfillment they have brought. I need no
other affirmation than to be called mother.
My children have taught me to forget myself, and through them, I have learned what
it means to be your child.

And the Lord said, I have pardoned according to thy word: But as truly as I live, all the earth shall be filled with the glory of the Lord.

Numbers 14:20–21

Lord, the best way I know to say thank you for your wonderful guidance is to try to be the kind of person you have taught me to be. Please continue to lift me up every day as I strive to be my best self.

MAY 13

Lord, you are the foundation of my life.
When circumstances shift and make my
world unsteady, you remain firm. When
threats of what lies ahead blow against the
framework of my thoughts, you are solid.
When I focus on your steadfastness, I realize
that you are my strength for the moment,
the one sure thing in my life. Because of you
I stand now, and I will stand tomorrow as
well, because you are there already.
Amen.

Blessed be the Lord, who daily loadeth us with benefits, even the God of our salvation.

Psalm 68:19

We thank thee, heav'nly Father,

For ev'ry earthly good,

For life, and health, and clothing,

And for our daily food.

O give us hearts to thank thee,

For ev'ry blessing sent,

And whatsoe'er thou sendest

Make us therewith content. Amen.

—Traditional hymn

*Open thy mouth for the dumb in the
cause of all such as are
appointed to destruction.*

Proverbs 31:8

Kathryn's six-year-old daughter Bailey
has a severe peanut allergy, but the school
Bailey attends did not have any protocols in
place should the girl experience an allergic
reaction. At first, the school administration
did not appreciate the severity of Bailey's
allergy, which is in fact life-threatening.
Kathryn's initial efforts to bring attention
to her daughter's condition were treated
dismissively; she had to dig deep to be the
firm, wise advocate her daughter's situation
demanded. Dear Lord, please help me to
be ready to speak up for those who cannot
speak for themselves. May I be a wise and
thoughtful advocate.

MAY 16

And he said, Draw not nigh hither: put off thy shoes from off thy feet, for the place whereon thou standest is holy ground.

Exodus 3:5

Help us to relax, Lord of calming seas, so that we don't become numb to the joy and awe of children, of family. For it is socially acceptable to kick off our shoes and tangibly feel the love. Make us alive, O God, to the holy grounds of life, and save us from taking these special places for granted.

In whom we have redemption through his blood, the forgiveness of sins, according to the riches of his grace.

Ephesians 1:7

Some days are better than others. Yesterday I was patient when my son forgot his books at school (again), when a coworker slighted me, and when I got the wrong change at the movie theater. Some days we are invited to forgive, and forgive again, and we can rise to the challenge. But there can be another kind of day, when I feel my temper rising and my brow lowering. On those days, I try to remember the fact that God has no reason to forgive us and yet he does so, again and again. He chooses to do so because of his grace. Dear Lord, may I always remember that forgiveness is a gift from you, and may I likewise, through your grace, be reminded to exercise forgiveness, joyfully, in my own affairs.

MAY 18

Count neither the hours nor the seconds
That filled your mind with doubts and fears.
Do not add up unhappy moments,
When pain and hardships brought you to tears.
Regard not days on faded calendars
That marked the passage of your years.
Instead, count heaven's blessings...
Grandchildren playing on the floor,
Old friends walking through the door,
White clouds drifting up above,
And, like a faithful timepiece, God's love.

*Blessed is he that considereth
the poor: the Lord will deliver him
in time of trouble.*

Psalm 41:1

Those who comfort others will themselves
be comforted. The Lord himself is as a
tender nurse to those who take care of
others. In fact, he "comforteth us in all
our tribulation, that we may be able to
comfort them which are in any trouble, by
the comfort wherewith we ourselves are
comforted of God" (2 Corinthians 1:4).

On our sickbed he comes to us, extending
grace to us as we have extended ourselves
to others. It is good to be gracious and kind
to those that are suffering; we see this is
the character of God himself. We imitate his
character to our own profit. As Jesus said,
"Inasmuch as ye have done it unto one of the
least of these my brethren, ye have done it
unto me" (Matthew 25:40).

And he changeth the times and the seasons: he removeth kings, and setteth up kings: he giveth wisdom unto the wise, and knowledge to them that know understanding.

Daniel 2:21

Lord, sometimes I feel you've blessed me with all kinds of knowledge that no one is interested in hearing! Help me know when and how to share your wisdom with others. Help me to show others your truth, rather than just talk about it. You taught us by living out the truth, Lord. Help us to do the same.

All praise to thee, my God, this night

For all the blessings of the light:

Keep me, O keep me, King of kings,

Beneath thine own almighty wings. Amen.

—Traditional evening prayer

MAY 22

A merry heart doeth good like a medicine: but a broken spirit drieth the bones.

Proverbs 17:22

Lord, how we thank you for the gift of laughter! Even in the midst of grief you send those happy memories that make us laugh and bring comfort to our souls. Laughter is so healing, Lord. It's reassuring to see so much evidence of your sense of humor. I feel confident there will be lots of laughter in heaven!

My mom died of cancer when I was still in college. She was diagnosed with a brain tumor in the spring, and was gone before Christmas. My dad was devastated and in his grief, withdrew from the world; he could not be there for us kids to lean on emotionally. It was a very difficult time in my life; what got me through was the support I received at the church in my college town. In what was probably the loneliest time in my life, I was nevertheless surrounded by love. Various members of the congregation invited me over for home-cooked meals or pizza-and-movie nights. These folks encouraged me that God was still there, and through their loving actions, I experienced God's grace. God is with us even when we feel alone.

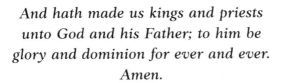

*And hath made us kings and priests
unto God and his Father; to him be
glory and dominion for ever and ever.
Amen.*

Revelation 1:6

I am an editor by trade and a fiction writer
by choice. For the past several years, I have
been working on a novel in the evening
and on weekends. Yesterday I made final
touches on what I believe is the final draft.
I closed my laptop, pulled on my jacket, and
went for a long walk. It was almost hard to
believe that the project that has consumed
my free time for so long was complete. I felt
a strange mix of relief and exhilaration, and
experienced a great welling of praise in my
heart. Lord, you have been with me every
step of the way, even when things seemed
unclear as to how to proceed with this book.
Now it is done! Thank you, thank you, for
being there. Thank you for helping me to
accomplish this.

Lord, may your kingdom come into my heart
to sanctify me, nourish me, and purify me.
How insignificant is the passing moment to
the eye without faith! But how important
each moment is to the eye enlightened
by faith! How can we deem insignificant
anything which has been caused by you?
Every moment and every event is guided by
you, and so contains your infinite greatness.
So, Lord, I glorify you in everything
that happens to me. In whatever manner
you make me live and die, I am content.
Everything is heaven to me, because all my
moments manifest your love.

—Jean-Pierre de Caussade,
"The Passing Moment"

MAY 26

Then said Jesus to those Jews which believed on him, If ye continue in my word, then are ye my disciples indeed; And ye shall know the truth, and the truth shall make you free.

John 8:31–32

What kind of freedom do you mean, Lord? There are people in jail cells in some countries because they have chosen to live according to your Word. Some of your other faithful followers struggle with illness or disability. So when you speak of freedom, you must mean something beyond a free body. I think you mean the spiritual freedom we enjoy in you. This freedom loosens any worldly bonds and holds the promise of eternal life in heaven. There the last vestiges of restraint will disappear, and our freedom will be complete.

For by grace are ye saved through faith; and that not of yourselves: it is the gift of God.

Ephesians 2:8

Dear Lord, we live in a broken world. We need your touch. Heal us of our prejudices, our sicknesses, our compulsions, our hatreds, and our shortsightedness. Help us to see people as you see them. For that matter, help us see ourselves as you see us. Teach us to treat life as the gift you meant it to be. Keep us safe. Make us whole. Give us love to spare and forgiveness that can only come from you. Amen.

MAY 28

I exhort therefore, that, first of all,
supplications, prayers, intercessions,
and giving of thanks,
be made for all men.

1 Timothy 2:1

Dear Lord, I live in a time and place of
entitlement. Sometimes, when others are
kind to me, generously offering their time or
assistance, I am in such a hurry that I take
their kindness as no more than my due. My
neighbor set aside his own work to help me
when I struggled in building a prefab kitchen
island equipped with hard-to-decipher
directions; my sister took off work and
traveled far to attend my son's middle school
graduation. Now I have a sturdy piece of
furniture, and my son's day was enriched by
the presence and support of his aunt. God,
these acts of love deserve to be recognized
as such. Please help me to remember to slow
down, appreciate, and thank those who are
generous to me.

MAY 29

Accept, O Lord, our thankful praises
For all thy goodness did bestow;
May it increase our faith and lead us
Our praise by godly lives to show,
That every deed and word may prove
We trust and own our Father's love.

Amen.

—Traditional prayer

*For the promise is unto you,
and to your children, and to all that
are afar off, even as many as the Lord
our God shall call.*

Acts 2:39

Lord, how we cling to your promise that
the Holy Spirit is always near to all who
believe in you. How comforting it is for us as
parents to know that our children have the
Holy Spirit to guide them and lead them into
a purposeful life. We praise you, Lord, for
your loving care for us and for our
children and grandchildren.

*In all thy ways acknowledge him, and
he shall direct thy paths.*

Proverbs 3:6

Lord, this is what I need today. I don't know
which direction to go or even what the
options are. I'm confused. I'm even afraid. So,
I fully and freely acknowledge that I need
your strength and direction. Save me from my
own wisdom and give me yours. I need you to
show me what to do and how to do it. Direct
my paths, Lord. Direct my paths.

JUNE

JUNE 1

Happy is he that hath the God of Jacob for his help, whose hope is in the Lord his God.

Psalm 146:5

The psalmist knew that with and through hope, we can find happiness in this life. Even though the principle of hope is a spiritual one, extending into eternity, it can also sustain us through the everyday challenges of life. We can, through hope, bring the strength of heaven into our homes, our workplaces, our minds, and our hearts. Our hope in God's promises empowers us with an eternal perspective.

Heal me, O Lord, and I shall be healed; save me, and I shall be saved: for thou art my praise.

Jeremiah 17:14

There is nothing the Lord won't do for me when I simply turn to him in praise. I have bad things happen just like anyone else, but his presence lifts my burdens and lightens my load. I turn to the Lord for healing of my body, mind, and spirit, knowing he will not deny me. I pray, dear Lord, to always walk in your presence. I pray you will forever be by my side as I journey through life's peaks and valleys. I pray, Lord, for the comfort and joy of knowing you will save me from my enemies and forgive me my sins. I can depend on you, Lord, to always have my back, even when those I count on have abandoned me.

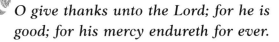

O give thanks unto the Lord; for he is good; for his mercy endureth for ever.

1 Chronicles 16:34

Mercy is the theme of David's song, right after the Ark of the Covenant has been returned to the people of God. It had been captured in battle but was now safely home. Perhaps you have something to celebrate today. Perhaps something meaningful and precious has been restored. Right now, give thanks to the Lord, for he is good. His loving-kindness never ends.

Cast thy burden upon the Lord, and he shall sustain thee: he shall never suffer the righteous to be moved.

Psalm 55:22

Lord, help me to be one of those people who cannot be moved. Sustain me with righteousness as I pray throughout this day, casting my burdens on you. You can carry them. I cannot. But because you carry them, I can stand firm, relying on you and your unfailing grace. This is the stability I need. This is your promise to your child.

For the bread of God is he which cometh down from heaven, and giveth life unto the world.

John 6:33

O Bread of Life, from day to day

Be thou our Comfort, Food, and Stay.

Amen.

—Traditional prayer

JUNE 6

The Lord is my shepherd;
I shall not want.

Psalm 23:1

Sometimes I feel abandoned, Lord. I feel
empty inside, and it's hard to connect with
myself, with others, and with the world. I
almost lose faith at these times, Lord. Please
stay with me and help me remember your
love, your light, and your peace.

Last year, my friend Cynthia was involved in a freak accident that killed her mother Susan and later her husband Mike. The three were heading to a family wedding when a wheel assembly from a passing truck hit their car. Because of where she was sitting, Cynthia survived with minor injuries. Cynthia didn't know it at the time, but she was three weeks pregnant. She gave birth to a healthy baby boy who is her pride and joy. "I don't think the accident was part of God's plan, but it helps to know that Mike lives on through my son and through the people who received Mike's organs," Cynthia says. God, when plans change in such life-altering ways, help us find silver linings.

JUNE 8

And it shall come to pass afterward, that I will pour out my spirit upon all flesh; and your sons and your daughters shall prophesy, your old men shall dream dreams, your young men shall see visions.

Joel 2:28

After Jesus' ascension, his disciples did as he had instructed and waited prayerfully for the promise. At Pentecost, ten days after Jesus had left them (promising he would return one day), the Spirit was poured out in an unmistakable way. The promise of God's presence with us by his Spirit is a gift that remains with us today. All who belong to Christ have the identifying mark or seal of God's Spirit working in their lives and are called daily to follow his direction and leading.

And the Lord, he it is that doth go before thee; he will be with thee, he will not fail thee, neither forsake thee: fear not, neither be dismayed.

Deuteronomy 31:8

Lord, give me the faith to take the next step, even when I don't know what lies ahead. Give me the assurance that even if I stumble and fall, you'll pick me up and put me back on the path. And give me the confidence that, even if I lose faith, you will never lose me.

When peace, like a river, attends my way.

When sorrows like sea billows roll;

Whatever my lot, you have taught me to say,

"It is well, it is well with my soul."

Though Satan should buffet,

Though trials should come,

Let this blest assurance control,

That Christ has regarded my helpless estate,

And has shed his own blood for my soul.

My sin—O the bliss of this glorious thought—

My sin, not in part, but the whole,

Is nailed to the cross, and I bear it no more,

Praise the Lord, praise the Lord, O my soul!

And, Lord, haste the day when

My faith shall be sight,

The clouds be rolled back as a scroll,

The trumpet shall sound and

The Lord shall descend,

Even so—it is well with my soul.

—Horatio G. Spafford

JUNE 11

I will call upon the Lord, who is worthy to be praised: so shall I be saved from mine enemies.

Psalm 18:3

Lord, make this our prayer, not just as individuals but as a nation. May we praise you; may our leaders praise you; may even our enemies praise you. You alone are worthy of such praise. There is safety in this kind of praise, the crying out of a nation who needs you and gives you the glory you deserve. Today we are grateful for your blessings and dependent on your mercy. Let us call on you and be glad.

JUNE 12

Blessed is the man that walketh not in the counsel of the ungodly, nor standeth in the way of sinners, nor sitteth in the seat of the scornful. But his delight is in the law of the Lord; and in his law doth he meditate day and night.

Psalm 1:1–2

My friends and I gossip. We like to give advice, too, even if we don't follow it ourselves. When I am with my friends, it is all too easy, Lord, to slip into these roles and find myself saying and doing things that aren't in accordance with your will.

I fall back into human ways, and then wonder why I feel out of balance. Help me to remember that life works best when I stay in alignment with your thoughts, Lord, asking myself throughout the day, "Is this my will at work here, or yours?"

JUNE 13

There hath no temptation taken you but such as is common to man: but God is faithful, who will not suffer you to be tempted above that ye are able; but will with the temptation also make a way to escape, that ye may be able to bear it.

1 Corinthians 10:13

Lord, sometime today I'm going to want to hedge the truth. I'm going to want to say something that springs from anger or bitterness, instead of love. Or I'm going to want to do something worse. Everybody does this. It is "common to man." But deliver me from temptation, Lord. You are faithful. You will come alongside me and whisper in my ear. Help me to hear you and obey you, because with your help, this temptation is not too much for me.

JUNE 14

And I say unto you, Ask, and it shall be given you; seek, and ye shall find; knock, and it shall be opened unto you. For everyone that asketh receiveth; and he that seeketh findeth; and to him that knocketh it shall be opened.

Luke 11:9–10

Jesus makes this precious promise right after he taught his disciples to pray what we know as the Lord's prayer. "Thy kingdom come," he prays. If this is our heart, we can ask, and it will be given. Such asking requires a kind of urgency, however, seeking and knocking with persistence and purpose, with the Father's will in our heart as we seek forgiveness and daily bread. For such prayers, the door of heaven opens.

JUNE 15

Thou wilt shew me the path of life:
in thy presence is fulness of joy;
at thy right hand there are
pleasures for evermore.

Psalm 16:11

Thank you, God of inspiration, for the times
when you guide me to take my place as
an example and a model for my children.
For you call us to be loving, tender, and
kind. Remind me that this call is more
than just creating a family, for the family is
Christianity in miniature.

JUNE 16

O God, who through the grace of thy Holy
Spirit, dost pour the gift of love into the
hearts of thy faithful people, grant unto
us health, both of mind and body, that we
may love thee with our whole strength, and
with entire satisfaction may perform those
things which are pleasing unto thee this day;
through Christ our Lord. Amen.

—11th-century prayer

And Jesus said unto them, Because of your unbelief: for verily I say unto you, If ye have faith as a grain of mustard seed, ye shall say unto this mountain, Remove hence to yonder place; and it shall remove; and nothing shall be impossible unto you.

Matthew 17:20

Lord, please help me to be more focused on the good in life and less focused on the bad. I know that faith is what brings good things into my world, but sometimes my faith gets a little shaky and I end up dwelling on the bad stuff going on around me. Show me how to open my heart back up and see things with new eyes. Change my perspective so that I can understand on a deeper level that what is happening to me is a blessing and not a curse. For this I am grateful, Lord.

JUNE 18

Regardless of what the future holds, I'm savoring all sorts of wondrous things I've been too busy to notice before. A thousand daily marvels bring a smile to my face. Through your grace, Lord, rather than thinking how sad it is that I missed them before, I'm delighted to be seeing, doing them now. These small wonders energize me, and for that I'm thankful. It's never too late to be a joyful explorer.

Forbearing one another, and forgiving one another, if any man have a quarrel against any: even as Christ forgave you, so also do ye.

Colossians 3:13

God empowers us to forgive one another. Natalie and her oldest friend Greta had a falling out when Natalie got wind of the fact that Greta had shared, with a mutual friend, something Natalie had told Greta in confidence. Though Greta's apology was sincere, Natalie's confidence in their friendship was shaken. Prayer and meditation helped Natalie talk honestly with Greta about what had transpired, and move forward with a relationship that was essentially strong. Dear God, friendship can be a grounding touchstone in this life. Just as you love and forgive us, may I love and forgive others, thus deepening the bonds of friendship.

JUNE 20

The day is done;
O God the Son,
Look down upon
Thy little one!
O Light of Light,
Keep me this night,
And shed round me
Thy presence bright.
I need not fear
If thou art near;
Thou art my savior
Kind and dear. Amen.
—Traditional evening prayer

My servant Moses is not so, who is faithful in all mine house.

Numbers 12:7

I miss my parents, both of whom died within the last 10 years, but each day I strive to keep them alive—in my heart and in the world—by emulating the way they lived their lives. On days when I struggle, I remember my mother's kindness, my father's acts of service. I remember the day my dad and I shared coffee and talked about the qualities he admired in others: "Faith," he said, without hesitation. "Faith in God, in one's own path. From faith springs generosity of spirit." He went on to say that in the Bible, the stories of faith as embodied by men such as Moses uplifted him. Dear God, may I persevere and have faith. Help me to remember that faithfulness is an attribute of great men like Moses, and within my reach as I strive to be my best self.

JUNE 22

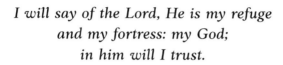

I will say of the Lord, He is my refuge
and my fortress: my God;
in him will I trust.

Psalm 91:2

What can I say, Lord? You created me. You
provide for me. You comfort me. And you
bless me, more than I deserve. But today,
Lord, protect me. You are my refuge and
fortress. Protect me from accidents and
enemies. Protect me from disease and
disaster. Protect me from myself, from rash
words and thoughts and from unwise choices
and their consequences. Protect me from all
this, Lord. You are my refuge and I trust you.

Blest feast of love divine!
'Tis grace that makes us free
To feed upon this bread and wine,
In memory Lord of thee.
That blood which flowed for sin,
In symbols here we see,
And feel the blessed pledge within
That we are loved by thee.

—Sir Edward Denny

Watch ye and pray, lest ye enter into temptation. The spirit truly is ready, but the flesh is weak.

Mark 14:38

I am grateful that every temptation has an escape hatch, Lord. I want to be a woman who is in the habit of looking for the way out of a tempting circumstance, not lingering in the snare zone. No matter how powerful the lure might be, help me resist the bait. Keep reminding me that your ways are best. They are filled with peace and satisfaction, and they never leave a trace of regret lingering in my soul.

Life can be lonely. When Sarah's husband was offered a job in Seattle, the couple decided to take the plunge and relocate. Sarah scored a job in their new city, too, but adjusting to the move has been challenging. She misses her group of friends; one night, talking to her sister, Ginny, on the phone, Sarah felt near tears. "I'm here," Ginny said. "Just a phone call away. And remember, God is your friend, too. He's always there." Dear God, you are my friend, always.

*Behold, I will bring it health and cure,
and I will cure them, and will reveal
unto them the abundance of
peace and truth.*

Jeremiah 33:6

Mental illness can be so devastating, Lord.
Few understand the heartaches involved
in diseases that carry no apparent physical
scars. Be with those friends, neighbors, and
family members who deal daily with difficult
situations of which we are often unaware.
Touch them with your special love, and let
them know that they can lean on you, Lord.
Ease their burdens, quell their sadness, and
calm their desperation. Bring peace and
healing to these households.

JUNE 27

For this new morning with its light,
For rest and shelter of the night,
For health and food, for love and friends.
For everything thy goodness sends,
We thank thee, dearest Lord. Amen.
—Traditional prayer

Behold the fowls of the air: for they sow not, neither do they reap, nor gather into barns; yet your heavenly Father feedeth them. Are ye not much better than they?

Matthew 6:26

Lord, help me not accuse you of being untrue when I don't get from you everything I want, for you have promised to meet all my needs. And when I learn to love you supremely and trust you wholly, my desires will find fulfillment in you.

JUNE 29

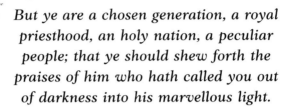

But ye are a chosen generation, a royal priesthood, an holy nation, a peculiar people; that ye should shew forth the praises of him who hath called you out of darkness into his marvellous light.

1 Peter 2:9

Dear God, thank you for calling us into light. So many people feel invisible and unloved. Think about your own life and ask if there is someone you've been ignoring or not appreciating. Too often, we think people don't need to hear how special and loved they are. Too often, we think others automatically know we cherish them. Today, I ask God to remind me as I go along to praise others and make them feel special. Not because I want to look good in God's eyes, but because they are special in my eyes, and they deserve to know. God, help me show my appreciation of others, especially those I sometimes forget about and take for granted.

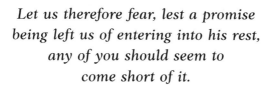

Let us therefore fear, lest a promise being left us of entering into his rest, any of you should seem to come short of it.

Hebrews 4:1

Father, it would be a great loss if I didn't enter the rest you promise, if I fell short of your plan and purpose for my life. Help me today to be faithful, trusting your eternal mercy, welcoming your coming, finding my security and hope in you. Your presence eases my fear. Help me rest in you when I am weary and believe in you when I am weak. Amen.

JULY

JULY 1

Let us therefore come boldly unto the throne of grace, that we may obtain mercy, and find grace to help in time of need.

Hebrews 4:16

New every morning is the love

Our wakening and uprising prove;

Through sleep and darkness safely brought,

Restored to life and power and thought.

New mercies, each returning day,

Hover around us while we pray;

New perils past, new sins forgiven,

New thoughts of God, new hopes of heaven.

—John Keble

JULY 2

And straightway the father of the child cried out, and said with tears, Lord, I believe; help thou mine unbelief.

Mark 9:24

I need to believe beyond the present darkness, for it threatens to stop me in my tracks. Steady me, God of infinite resources, as I collect my beliefs like candles to light and move through this dark tunnel of doubt and uncertainty. Inspire me to add new truths as they reveal themselves in my life. Along the way, help my unbelief.

JULY 3

God, today I ask for strength—not for myself, but for others I care about. There are couples that need strength to get past some conflict in their relationships. Cover them with your overwhelming love. There are teenagers, still figuring out who they are, who need strength to withstand temptation. Shore up their souls. There are single parents working night and day to care for their families. Guard their health and refresh their energy. There are senior citizens who need strength to do the things they easily used to do. Give them grace to live mightily for you. All around me are people with emotional wounds and spiritual struggles, those who feel ill-equipped and overwhelmed. Support them with your power for your eternal glory.

JULY 4

Stand fast therefore in the liberty wherewith Christ hath made us free, and be not entangled again with the yoke of bondage.

Galatians 5:1

I love the freedoms I enjoy as your child, Father. I also deeply appreciate the freedoms I enjoy as a citizen of a free country. Both citizenships—my heavenly one and my earthly one—call for responsible living on my part, but these responsibilities are really a joy and a privilege. Help me to always keep this in the forefront of my mind as I make choices each day.

JULY 5

Surely he shall deliver thee from the snare of the fowler, and from the noisome pestilence.

Psalm 91:3

Dear God, I am surrounded by deception and disease. Only you can deliver me. And you will. Help me let this sink in, Lord. You are my deliverer, a place of safety when others try to trap me and a place of healing when circumstances plague me. Comfort me with this assurance: Surely you will deliver me. That will always be enough.

JULY 6

And our hope of you is stedfast, knowing, that as ye are partakers of the sufferings, so shall ye be also of the consolation.

2 Corinthians 1:7

Heavenly Father, I hold up to you my child who is ill. While I think everything will be okay, I worry, and stress and lack of sleep only exacerbate that worry. I know, though, that you love my child even more than I do—even if that seems impossible to me! You want what's best for all of us. During this dark and restless and feverish night, help me let go of my fear as I place my trust and my hope in you.

JULY 7

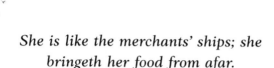

She is like the merchants' ships; she bringeth her food from afar.

Proverbs 31:14

The recession hit our family hard, but I'm proud of the way my husband and I stepped up and managed what could have been a scary situation. I've worked outside the home since our children were small, but after the market collapse, my husband was laid off and we both took on a series of extra jobs to make ends meet. It wasn't always easy, but together, we have stayed on top of the bills and kept things stable for the kids. I see the same grit in my sister, who is a young widow with a son of her own. "Women are strong," I tell her, and I mean it. Dear Lord, thank you for this strength. Women are providers!

Behold, I have done according to thy words: lo, I have given thee a wise and an understanding heart; so that there was none like thee before thee, neither after thee shall any arise like unto thee.

1 Kings 3:12

God, thank you for giving me a kind heart and a wise mind. There was a time when my friends didn't want to spend much time with me because I was always too busy doling out advice and not simply being a loving friend. I thought I was helping, but was instead being annoying. I understood over time a real friend offers unconditional love before giving any advice, no matter how wise the advice. My friends noticed the change in me, and I noticed a new depth to my relationships. Love and wisdom go together, and those who have both, shine.

Judge not, and ye shall not be judged: condemn not, and ye shall not be condemned: forgive, and ye shall be forgiven.

Luke 6:37

Dear God, I know that I have wronged others over the course of the years. I pray that those moments are long forgotten, and if they are not, I pray that I might somehow make them right. I truly forgive anyone who has wronged me, letting go of any grudges or hurtful feelings. And I pray that as I forgive, so may I be forgiven. Amen.

Whate'er I do, things great or small
Whate'er I speak or frame.
Thy glory may I seek in all,
Do all in Jesus' name.
My Father, for his sake I pray.
Thy child accept and bless
And lead me by thy grace today
In paths of righteousness. Amen.
—Traditional morning prayer

JULY 11

And as ye would that men should do to you, do ye also to them likewise.

Luke 6:31

Yesterday I got into a car accident. It was my fault—I was in a hurry and tried to cross an intersection just as yellow turned to red—but I felt defensive and berated the driver whose car I had clipped. I was embarrassed when the driver met my bluster with calm grace; later, after I'd regained my composure, it also struck me how much I appreciated being spoken to respectfully, though I myself had been less than gracious. The other driver's consideration made an impression, and when I told my wife about it, she smiled gently and observed, "That guy was probably just treating you the way he wished you'd treat him!" God, remind me to treat others as I would want them to treat me.

JULY 12

Let us therefore desire nothing else, wish for nothing else, and let nothing please and delight us except our Creator and Redeemer, and Savior, the only true God, who is full of good, who alone is good, . . . and from whom, and through whom, and in whom is all mercy, all grace, all glory of all penitents and of the just, and of all the blessed rejoicing in heaven.

—St. Francis of Assisi

Be not overcome of evil, but overcome evil with good.

Romans 12:21

God, teach me to have the courage to act in the world as you wish me to. Help me find a way to push through the challenges that arise in my path, and show me how to overcome evil with love and compassion. Help me to stand tall against fear and stay in the light. Amen.

JULY 14

For whosoever exalteth himself shall be abased; and he that humbleth himself shall be exalted.

Luke 14:11

Lord, we live in a world where there is a great clamoring for power and glory. Greed runs rampant, and time and again we see the inglorious results of someone's unethical attempts to climb to the top. Protect us from such fruitless ambition, Lord. For we know that it is only when we humble ourselves that you will lift us up higher than we could ever have imagined. All power and glory is yours, forever and ever. Until we acknowledge that truth, we will never be great in anyone's eyes—especially yours.

*Thou shalt have no
other gods before me.*

Exodus 20:3

Lord, please keep me from falling into
the trap of placing any other human
on a pedestal. Even the most spiritual-
seeming religious leaders are riddled with
imperfection; they struggle with sin, just as I
do. You alone are perfect and pure, and you
alone are worthy of my adoration. I promise
I will not follow anyone else, no matter how
spiritually enlightened they may seem. There
is no one like you, and you are the only one
who will ever have my full devotion.

O thou of God the Father

The true Eternal Son,

Of whom the Word declareth

That thou with him art one;

Thou art the bright and Morning Star,

Beyond all other radiance

Thy glory streams afar.

—Elisabethe Creutziger,
trans. Catherine Winkworth

Fear thou not; for I am with thee: be not dismayed; for I am thy God: I will strengthen thee; yea, I will help thee; yea, I will uphold thee with the right hand of my righteousness.

—Isaiah 41:10

No matter what my ears may hear

Or what my eyes may see,

There's nothing for me to fear, Lord;

You're always here with me.

Two are better than one; because they have a good reward for their labour.

Ecclesiastes 4:9

Nicole's elderly mom, who has been struggling to keep up her house, is preparing the home for sale, and Nicole offered to help with yard work. After one day of working the large, overgrown property, Nicole confessed to a friend that she was feeling overwhelmed. Her friend not only offered to help, but showed up with her two cheerful sons in tow. "Working together, we had the yard in shape within a day!" Nicole enthused. "It was fun!" Dear Lord, you put friends in my life, and I thank you; working together, my friends and I can move mountains. Many together can accomplish much, and there is joy in the sharing!

JULY 19

And brought in the offerings and the tithes and the dedicated things faithfully: over which Cononiah the Levite was ruler, and Shimei his brother was the next.

2 Chronicles 31:12

Dear God, money is tight this summer: Our old refrigerator gave out sooner than we might have hoped and replacing it was an unexpected expense, as was the series of doctor's visits when I strained my shoulder. Last Sunday, the ushers passed the offering plate and I am ashamed to admit that I held back: After all, I justified, I am spread thin this month! Rather than contributing something, I contributed nothing, and in my frugality, I lost both connection and the sense of continuity I strive for in my spiritual life. Lord, giving to you is not only an act of faith (because I am giving to someone unseen), but also something I should do faithfully. Thank you for helping me to remember this.

Blest be the tie that binds

Our hearts in Christian love;

The fellowship of kindred minds

Is like to that above.

Before our Father's throne

We pour our ardent prayers;

Our fears, our hopes, our aims are one,

Our comforts and our cares.

When we asunder part,

It gives us inward pain,

But we shall still be joined in heart,

And hope to meet again.

—Rev. John Fawcett

*The steps of a good man are ordered
by the Lord: and he delighteth in his
way. Though he fall, he shall not
be utterly cast down: for the Lord
upholdeth him with his hand.*

Psalm 37:23–24

Stumbling happens. Don't I know it! I can
get bummed out just by reviewing my
mistakes and mess-ups from yesterday. But
thankfully, I don't need to! God has hold
of my hand. My worst blunders—even
if they've been truly harmful to myself
or others—are not the end of the world.
God will bring a new day, a fresh start, a
redeemed relationship, a restored soul.

JULY 22

For whosoever shall give you a cup of water to drink in my name, because ye belong to Christ, verily I say unto you, he shall not lose his reward.

Mark 9:41

Our kindness to others has eternal consequences. This is true even of small kindnesses, a cup of water in Jesus' name. A smile will also count, especially when offered to someone on the margins of life, someone overlooked and perhaps misunderstood. The people who care for you in this way will also be rewarded. Wouldn't it be great if we all extended such kindness to each other?

JULY 23

We love him, because he first loved us.

1 John 4:19

Lord, thank you for heirlooms. The rocking chair where I remember sitting on Grandma's lap, and then rocking my own child, is now being passed down. I cherish the thought of every moment I will hold my own grandchild. I thank you for all these connections to the past and these legacies of love, for all love flows ultimately from you.

*Humble yourselves in the sight of the
Lord, and he shall lift you up.*

James 4:10

You have to go down to get up. It's a paradox
worth celebrating. As we humble ourselves
before the Lord, he lifts us up. Obviously,
we don't get that far when we try to do
it ourselves. What's really amazing is the
heights are greater and the view is clearer
when he does it. Only then do we see how
small our vision was and how meager our
efforts were. He always has a better plan
than the one we made in pride.

Brethren, I count not myself to have apprehended: but this one thing I do, forgetting those things which are behind, and reaching forth unto those things which are before, I press toward the mark for the prize of the high calling of God in Christ Jesus.

Philippians 3:13–14

After graduating high school, Anna took a year off to work and earn money for university. "Sometimes it's a little lonely," Anna admits. "Many of my friends have already gone on to college." On low days, Anna feels left behind, but then she reminds herself that this is her path, it's a good one, and that God supports her, always. "God has my back," Anna says simply. "That comforts me." God, you are my best coach! I don't need to reach higher alone; thank you for being there to inspire me.

All people that on earth do dwell,

Sing to the Lord with cheerful voice.

Serve him with joy, his praises tell,

Come now before him and rejoice!

Know that the Lord is God indeed;

He formed us all without our aid.

We are the flock he comes to feed,

The sheep who by his hand were made.

O enter then his gates with joy,

Within his courts his praise proclaim.

Let thankful songs your tongues employ.

O bless and magnify his name.

Trust that the Lord our God is good,

His mercy is forever sure.

His faithfulness at all times stood

And shall from age to age endure.

—William Kethe

*Now therefore fear ye not: I will
nourish you, and your little ones.
And he comforted them, and spake
kindly unto them.*

Genesis 50:21

Money is a big issue for most people, and
I am no exception. Either we don't have
enough, or we worry about losing what we
have. We are afraid of being left homeless
and destitute. But God promises he will
comfort and nourish us, with material things
and things no amount of money can buy.
God tells us not to be afraid. Dear God, I
pray to worry less, and have more faith in
your promise of prosperity. Even when my
wallet looks empty, I know that blessings are
happening in the unseen and will soon be
made manifest. You never fail to sustain and
support me, God. I pray for your care and
comfort in good financial times and in bad.

Thou art wearied in the greatness of thy way; yet saidst thou not, There is no hope: thou hast found the life of thine hand; therefore thou wast not grieved.

Isaiah 57:10

Galvanize me into prevention, intervention, and rebuilding your world, Creator God. Kids need fixers, not just worriers and those prone to panic. They need to hear plans, not just alarms. Let hope, not fear, be the last word in the bedtime stories I tell.

God, there are so many times throughout my day when my words don't match my actions. I know others are looking to me to be an example of living rightly, but sometimes I just need help keeping my integrity. Help me to not break promises, to watch what I commit to—or overcommit to—especially if I know in my heart I cannot come through. Most of all, match my outer actions to my inner thoughts so that I am walking the talk. I get frustrated when others don't come through with their promises, and I ask that you help me to not become one of those people myself.

JULY 30

My shepherd is the living Lord:
Now shall my needs be well supplied;
His loving care and holy word
Will be my safety and my guide.
In pastures where salvation grows
He makes me feed, he gives me rest;
There living water gently flows,
And food is given, divinely blest.
Though I walk through the gloomy vale
Where death and all its terrors are,
My heart and hope shall never fail:
My shepherd holds me in his care.
Amid the darkness and the deeps,
God is my comfort, God my stay;
His staff supports my feeble steps,
His rod directs my doubt-filled way.
Surely the mercies of the Lord
Attend his household all their days;
There will I dwell, to hear his word,
To seek his face, to sing his praise.

—Isaac Watts

JULY 31

Verily, verily, I say unto you, He that believeth on me hath everlasting life. I am that bread of life. Your fathers did eat manna in the wilderness, and are dead. This is the bread which cometh down from heaven, that a man may eat thereof, and not die. I am the living bread which came down from heaven: if any man eat of this bread, he shall live for ever: and the bread that I will give is my flesh, which I will give for the life of the world.

John 6:47–51

Nothing fills us like the bread from heaven. Jesus says here there is spiritual food: lasting and alive. He is himself the bread of life, the bread that satisfies us in this life and the next one. The eternal life that he gives is costly, though. He gives his own flesh for the life of the world, a life that does not end. Believe in me, he says. That's the bread of life.

AUGUST

AUGUST 1

Write thy blessed name, O Lord, upon my heart, there to remain so indelibly engraven, that no prosperity, no adversity shall ever move me from thy love. Be thou to me a strong tower of defence, a comforter in tribulation, a deliverer in distress, a very present help in trouble, and a guide to heaven through the many temptations and dangers of this life. Amen.

—Thomas à Kempis

AUGUST 2

But even the very hairs of your head are all numbered. Fear not therefore: ye are of more value than many sparrows.

Luke 12:7

If God creates us in his image, he must value us. Then why do so many people in the world today suffer from loneliness, depression, and low self-worth? I myself have struggled with low self-esteem, when I felt powerless and unable to cope. But God made us in his image, and we are worthy of all of his blessings and his love. He promised us this and he always keeps his word. God, help us to recognize our inherent worth, and to realize that we are loved. Help us know our value as your beloved children.

AUGUST 3

Draw nigh to God, and he will draw nigh to you. Cleanse your hands, ye sinners; and purify your hearts, ye double minded.

James 4:8

Be all in today. Clean up your act. Clean up your thoughts. Draw near to God, boldly and completely. There is no place for second thoughts or tentative commitments. It is all in, all the time: seeking God, depending on his strength, believing his promises. If you do this, God will draw near to you. That's all you really need.

AUGUST 4

And they which went before rebuked him, that he should hold his peace: but he cried so much the more, Thou son of David, have mercy on me.

Luke 18:39

The college track was not fruitful or satisfying for Jenn, but when she told friends she was thinking of leaving school to start her own business, cutting hair, they discouraged her. "I let myself be convinced that it was foolish to stray from a certain path," Jenn says now. It took another difficult school year for her to decide she was ready to strike out on her own. Now she's not only successful in her business, but personally fulfilled. God, Luke's story of the blind man fills me with hope. Thank you for reminding me that I mustn't let others tell me "what I can't do."

AUGUST 5

Pitching in on the caregiving rotation for my elderly aunt was not something I initially perceived as a blessing, but as a gift I was giving to my aunt and my cousin. Still, God, I thank you for this opportunity to grow, to give, and to learn. The work of caregiving can be stressful and emotionally wearing, but I am learning that when I trust in you and let you work through me, I am able to do the work with a generous heart.

AUGUST 6

And whatsoever ye shall ask in my name, that will I do, that the Father may be glorified in the Son. If ye shall ask any thing in my name, I will do it.

John 14:13–14

Lord Jesus, it is so easy to seek comfort from material things—from a new car or sofa, from a trip to the mall or from the movies. But you are not found in worldly things. The only true source of everlasting comfort is your love, the living water you offer us from your very lips. Let me remember to seek first your will, perfect and divine. It is only then that my weary heart will rest and find sanctuary. Amen.

AUGUST 7

Bless the Lord, O my soul: and all that is within me, bless his holy name.

Psalm 103:1

Holy God, you have shown me light and life. You are stronger than any natural power. Accept the words from my heart that struggle to reach you. Accept the silent thoughts and feelings that are offered to you. Clear my mind of the clutter of useless facts. Bend down to me, and lift me in your arms. Make me holy as you are holy. Give me a voice to sing of your love to others.

AUGUST 8

But love ye your enemies, and do good, and lend, hoping for nothing again; and your reward shall be great, and ye shall be the children of the Highest: for he is kind unto the unthankful and to the evil.

Luke 6:35

An amazing thing about God is his kindness to people who are ungrateful and even evil. Even on your worst day, you can receive mercy and grace. But it is clearly not the best option. Jesus says instead we should love our enemies and do good, without expectation or self-interest. Then we will be known as the children of God. And if he is even kind to those who do not love him, imagine the rewards for those who do.

Light serene of holy glory
From the Immortal Father poured,
Holy Thou, O blessed Jesus,
Holy, blessed, Christ the Lord.
Now we see the sun descending,
Now declines the evening light,
And in hymns we praise the Father,
Son and Spirit, God of Might.
—Early Christian hymn, trans. John Brownlie

AUGUST 10

Lord, a friend is going through an incredibly difficult time. Sometimes even well-meaning words can grate on raw nerves, and I don't want to say the wrong thing or, in trying to make things better, minimize her pain. When I am with her, please give me the right words to say at the right time—whether they are words of encouragement, commiseration, or understanding. And if what she needs is simply a comforting hug while she cries, let me be present to her. Sometimes silence is the best gift we have to offer.

AUGUST 11

For God, who commanded the light to shine out of darkness, hath shined in our hearts, to give the light of the knowledge of the glory of God in the face of Jesus Christ.

2 Corinthians 4:6

Lord, your Word is so alive—so vibrant— that it almost seems illuminated when I am reading it. When I am troubled, opening the Bible is like turning on a comforting light in a dark, gloomy room. Thank you, Lord, for loving us so much that you gave us your wisdom to illuminate our lives.

AUGUST 12

To every thing there is a season,
and a time to every purpose
under the heaven.

Ecclesiastes 3:1

You don't need to run a marathon. Just
take one step at a time. Go out in faith and
let God guide you. There is a season for
everything, and God has perfect timing. Just
listen and when he tells you to move, move!

For we dare not make ourselves of the number, or compare ourselves with some that commend themselves: but they measuring themselves by themselves, and comparing themselves among themselves, are not wise.

2 Corinthians 10:12

When Miranda first tried yoga, she was intimidated by her classmates, some of whom had been practicing for years. But her instructor, Jane, helped put things in perspective. "Jane reminded me that yoga isn't about comparing oneself to others," Miranda says. "It's about my own progress. I may never be as flexible as some of my classmates, but I'm proud of the improvements I've seen in my own abilities." Dear Lord, sometimes I fall into the trap of comparing myself to others, and that's a slippery slope. Help me to focus on my own progress, my own heart—not someone else's.

AUGUST 14

*Knowing this, that the trying of your
faith worketh patience.*

James 1:3

"I don't like challenge, but it does build character," Felicia shares during a quick break at work. Felicia's mother has been diagnosed with ALS; Felicia, a single mom, works full-time. She and her siblings are trying to navigate managing care for their mom while keeping their own lives under control. She shakes her head with a wry laugh. "I keep telling myself, the strength I'm tapping into will serve me well in other areas of my life, too!" Dear Lord, this has been a trying time. Help me to remember that adversity builds character; help me to remember that the events of this year may, ultimately, make me better suited to succeed.

AUGUST 15

Help me understand, Lord, that the courage I am praying for is not dry-eyed stoicism and perky denial. Courage is not hiding my feelings, even from you, and putting on a brave false face. Rather it is facing facts, weighing options, and moving ahead. No need to waste precious time pretending.

AUGUST 16

God, hear my prayer. Bless me with patience
and a steadfast heart to help me get through
such emotionally trying times. Heal the
wounds of my heart and soul with the
soothing balm of your comforting presence,
that I may be able to love and to live again.
Amen.

AUGUST 17

And when ye stand praying, forgive, if ye have ought against any: that your Father also which is in heaven may forgive you your trespasses.

Mark 11:25

When my dear wife died of cancer, many friends stepped forward, but some—even friends I hold dear—disappointed me by not being there for me as much as I might have hoped. Death is a frightening thing, my wife's death was untimely, and I tried to remember that people's lives are complex. Sometimes, I imagine, my expectations were simply too high. And yet it was painful for me to understand that some loved ones could not, for whatever reason, be there for me in my grief. It was only through prayer that I gained a measure of relief, perspective, and calm. God, thank you for always being there to listen to me. Prayer puts me in the right frame of mind to forgive others and, sometimes, to forgive myself.

AUGUST 18

Now to that God, who has suffered so much for us, who at one giving has conferred on us so many good things, and will yet confer so many more, to this God let every creature who is in heaven or upon the earth, in the sea or in the depth of the abyss, render praise, glory, honor and blessing. He is himself our virtue and our strength. He alone is good, lofty, almighty, admirable, and glorious; the only holy, worthy of praise and blessed through ages of ages. Amen.

—St. Francis of Assisi

AUGUST 19

Labour not for the meat which perisheth, but for that meat which endureth unto everlasting life, which the Son of man shall give unto you: for him hath God the Father sealed.

John 6:27

Heavenly Father, I seek the nourishment that comes from true inner strength. I know that food fuels the body, but my spirit needs the fuel of deep and abiding peace and the understanding that I'm never alone in the world. With you, Father, I have that foundation of strength to feed me from the inside out. I'm able to go forth and face any challenge and overcome any obstacle. I ask that you continue to nourish me with resilience, fortitude, and faith.

AUGUST 20

But exhort one another daily, while it is called To day; lest any of you be hardened through the deceitfulness of sin.

Hebrews 3:13

Robin loves her brother Jim; she also knows he struggles with a gambling addiction. The siblings were driving together to a wedding, and their travels took them past a casino. Jim wanted to stop. Robin didn't want conflict, but she stood firm. "It was hard for me to confront him, but we actually had a good talk," Robin says now. "And we didn't go to the casino. That day, Jim needed me to help him do the right thing." Dear God, please be with me. When I see someone tempted or vulnerable, help me to reach out and offer encouragement.

AUGUST 21

If any of you lack wisdom, let him ask of God, that giveth to all men liberally, and upbraideth not; and it shall be given him.

James 1:5

I recently took on a new position at work. It's a stretch for me, and while I welcome the change (my previous duties no longer challenged me), I am also fearful of failure. My new position will require a steep learning curve, and demands that I oversee a number of employees. What if I can't master the material? What if I don't have what it takes to manage others wisely? But I must remember that God is always there to help me. He can increase wisdom—not just spiritually, but in all ways. Dear Lord, please be with me as I challenge myself to develop intellectually and master new skills. Please help me to stay sharp, and to grow as a person, with energy and grace.

AUGUST 22

*Denying ungodliness and worldly lusts,
we should live soberly, righteously,
and godly, in this present world.*

Titus 2:12

Have you ever met someone who solely
defines themselves by their possessions?
Though society may seem to reward those
who achieve their self-worth from having
the "right" car, or the biggest house, these
individuals are, at the root of it, unhappy
people. Material gain in and of itself is,
ultimately, an empty victory. Don't be that
person. Don't let your worldly interests cloud
your true sense of self. Dear God, may what
really matters define who I am as a person!

AUGUST 23

I offer up unto thee my prayers and intercessions, for those especially who have in any matter hurt, grieved, or found fault with me, or who have done me any damage or displeasure.

For all those also whom, at any time, I may have vexed, troubled, burdened, and scandalized, by words or deeds, knowingly or in ignorance; that thou wouldst grant us all equally pardon for our offences against each other.

Take away from our hearts, O Lord, all suspiciousness, indignation, wrath, and contention, and whatsoever may hurt charity, and lessen brotherly love.

Have mercy, O Lord, have mercy on those that crave thy mercy, give grace unto them that stand in need thereof, and make us such as that we may be worthy to enjoy thy grace, and go forward to life eternal. Amen.

—Thomas à Kempis

*And my tongue shall speak of thy
righteousness and of thy praise
all the day long.*

Psalm 35:28

In a church or family, praising can have
the nice effect of building up others
and spreading cheer. In our house, we'll
occasionally indulge in what we call "love
bombardment": Someone will get singled out
for a blitz of praise, during which everyone
else in the house heaps compliments upon
the designated recipient. We usually focus on
someone who's had a long or challenging day.
It doesn't take long for everyone to be caught
up in laughter, and the object of affection
gets a nice boost. Everyone needs a lift sometimes, and taking part in praise bombardment
has proven, in our house at least, to be a
balm for all concerned. Dear Lord, help me to
remember that attitudes are infectious.

*And I will walk among you,
and will be your God, and
ye shall be my people.*

Leviticus 26:12

How amazing you are, O Lord! You are
all-powerful and all-knowing, and yet you
promise to walk with me. You sent Jesus,
your son, to live as one of us, to walk among
us. You claim us as your own. When I am
feeling downcast, let me remember that the
Lord of the universe chooses to love me.
I thank you and praise you!

AUGUST 26

Where no counsel is, the people fall: but in the multitude of counselors there is safety.

Proverbs 11:14

Mandy has always prided herself on her independence. But when buying a new home, she sought the advice of trusted friends: Ken, who works in construction and could spot structural issues, and Denise, who has a good head for finance and helped Mandy navigate the paperwork. With their support, she found a solid house at a price she could afford. "It's hard for me to rely on others," Mandy confessed. "But my friends helped me make a wise choice."

Dear Lord, grant me the humility to seek— and listen to!—the counsel of others. Grant me the wisdom to surround myself with wise friends.

Sometimes when I am going through a hard time, I have friends or family members who are willing to offer help, to share my burden for a while, but I have a hard time accepting their help because I feel I should be strong and handle it alone. Father God, please help me balance independence and community. Please help me remember that part of being in a loving relationship is accepting love—that in accepting love, I accept you more deeply in my life, for you are love!

AUGUST 28

I acknowledge my sin unto thee, and mine iniquity have I not hid. I said, I will confess my transgressions unto the Lord; and thou forgavest the iniquity of my sin.

Psalm 32:5

Confessing our sin to God is like bursting into cool, refreshing air after being stuck a long time in a stifling, hot room. It frees our soul from the suffocating misery of pride, guilt, and pretense. Best of all, "coming clean" about our wrongdoing is the way back to right relationship with God. His merciful love grants us the forgiveness we so desperately need.

AUGUST 29

Behold, I stand at the door, and knock: if any man hear my voice, and open the door, I will come in to him, and will sup with him, and he with me.

Revelation 3:20

Jesus says if we just open the door we can dine together. But not every visitor is welcome. Some we like to see come, and some we like to see go. "Remember me, O Lord, with the favour that thou bearest unto thy people: O visit me with thy salvation," Psalm 106:4 says.

But sometimes we do not want a visitor. When Job says, "What is man . . . that thou shouldest visit him every morning, and try him every moment?" he is at least a little annoyed (Job 7:17–18). Our welcome depends on a prepared heart. But he will knock. "God will surely visit you," Joseph told his brothers (Genesis 50:24). It is best to be ready.

AUGUST 30

For thou art my lamp, O Lord: and the Lord will lighten my darkness.

2 Samuel 22:29

Heavenly Father, I ask for your bright presence. When I leave you behind and try to go about my day without your guidance, Lord, it's like groping around in the dark. I stub my heart on relational issues. I trip over my ego. I bump into walls of frustration. I fall down the steps of my foolish choices. How much better to seek the light of your presence first thing and enjoy the benefit of having you illuminate each step of my day!

AUGUST 31

Dear Lord, in this time of back-to-school excitement, I pray for all children who are returning to the classroom. May they have a productive year of education and friendship. Please grant teachers patience and fulfillment, and bless all maintenance workers, administrators, principals, and aides who work behind the scenes. I pray especially for those who are apprehensive about this return—non-traditional learners, children who are being bullied, and children and staff who are dealing with weighty issues at home. May they feel a sense of your presence as they walk into the school each day.

SEPTEMBER

SEPTEMBER 1

Thank you for my community. As I run my errands and conduct my business, let me remember to be grateful for everyone who helps me. From a clerk at the store to the police officer keeping me safe, my community is filled with people who help others. Thank you, Lord, for putting these people in my life and for giving me the chance to know them. May I always work to make my community a better place.

This day is holy unto our Lord: neither be ye sorry; for the joy of the Lord is your strength.

Nehemiah 8:10

Lord, my heart aches for my friend, who is undergoing chemotherapy. How it saps her energy, Lord. Sometimes it seems the cure is more devastating than the disease. Stay close to her in this time of healing, Lord. Bring her comfort, and fill her with the knowledge that she can find hope in you. I know you will lend her the strength she needs to get through this trying time.

Gracious Father, you are at work day and night on our behalf as you watch over us. We want our children to know that work is a noble thing, a necessary part of life, and that we are all fellow workers with you.

We wish to teach the children that no matter how small the chore, it can and should be done to your glory.

We thank you, Lord, for the opportunity for honest labor, and we present ourselves to you as workers who need not be ashamed. Grant that our attitudes spill over into our children's lives so they, too, may know the satisfaction of earning their daily bread.

SEPTEMBER 4

And we know that all things work together for good to them that love God, to them who are the called according to his purpose.

Romans 8:28

"Sometimes I get discouraged!" Ava says with a laugh. She's talking about her efforts to be more organized at work. "My desk still gets really messy sometimes—I'm terrible about filing things away and I get these piles of paper everywhere—but I remind myself that I'm on the right path. My performance at work has improved overall." She smiles wryly. "There is hope!" Dear Lord, help me to have confidence that I am on the right path as I strive to grow as a person.

SEPTEMBER 5

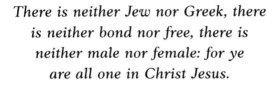

There is neither Jew nor Greek, there is neither bond nor free, there is neither male nor female: for ye are all one in Christ Jesus.

Galatians 3:28

It's easy to love a friend for all the things we have in common. It's harder, but much more valuable, to love the things that set us apart from one another. Learning to appreciate our differences brings a new level of intimacy to our relationships with others.

SEPTEMBER 6

O almighty and merciful Father, who pourest thy benefits upon us, forgive the unthankfulness with which we have requited thy goodness. We have remained before thee with dead and senseless hearts, unkindled with love of thy gentle and enduring goodness. Turn thou us, O merciful Father, and so shall we be turned. Make us with our whole heart to hunger and thirst after thee, and with all our longing to desire thee. Make us with our whole heart to serve thee alone and with all our zeal to seek those things which are well-pleasing in thy sight; for the sake of thine only begotten Son, to whom with thee and the Holy Ghost be all honor and glory, for ever and ever. Amen.

—St. Anselm

Children, obey your parents in all things: for this is well pleasing unto the Lord.

Colossians 3:20

Dear Lord, I am officially in the "Sandwich Generation," raising my own children while helping my parents navigate the challenges of aging. Mom and Dad, who have always been there for me, now need me in new ways. Dad has developed Parkinson's, and Mom's arthritis is getting worse. My husband and I are devoted to helping them with practical matters like getting to the doctor, cleaning their home, and buying groceries, and I have recently started bringing my older daughter along when we run errands with Mom. The challenges my folks face make me keenly aware of life's cycles of loss and change; I know my daughter feels it, too. But my hope is that these dates with Mom might be a way to demonstrate to my daughter what respect for elders can mean. Aging is a part of being, and compassion is an important lesson. Dear God, help me set the right example for my children through my relationship with my own parents.

Which when they had read, they rejoiced for the consolation.

Acts 15:31

In the digital age, Tamara still writes letters to send by post. She writes to her brother. She writes to a favorite aunt. "Sure, I use email, too," she shares. "And I text. But I know I'm always thrilled when I get a 'real' letter in my mailbox, rather than just bills and junk mail. There is permanence to a written note, on lovely paper, that gives me a lift. I hope my letters bring the same kind of joy." Dear Lord, written words have lasting power. May what I write bring solace and joy!

Father, I realize now that even people
of faith have different struggles with
discouragement and depression. It's a
relief to realize that I'm not the only one.
But where do I go from here? I need your
wisdom and guidance. I guess this time
of praying is the best place to begin. Just
being reminded that you are near keeps me
from the despair of feeling all alone, and it's
comforting to feel so heard and understood
when I'm talking with you. I need you to
help me through this day, Father.
Just this day. I'll take them one at
a time with you.

And whatsoever ye do in word or deed, do all in the name of the Lord Jesus, giving thanks to God and the Father by him.

Colossians 3:17

When Noelle first saw the Victorian house that eventually became her home, she knew she had work to do. The house had good bones but had fallen into disrepair, and for months she sanded and painted; her brother even helped her tear out a wall. There were unexpected setbacks. But she prevailed, and now her home is comfortable and a place of refuge. "I thank God," Noelle says. "He gave me the strength to realize my vision." Dear God, may I always remember to put you at the center of my achievements!

SEPTEMBER 11

Even every one that is called by my name: for I have created him for my glory, I have formed him; yea, I have made him.

Isaiah 43:7

When Angela's son Kevin left for college, Angela was surprised to discover the extent to which she felt at loose ends. "I was still working as a nurse then," she remembers, "but with Kevin successfully out in the world, I felt a lack of motivation." Reexamining her faith helped. "I began by thanking God for Kevin's happiness—the way he was spreading his wings," she says now. "Glorifying God in this way restored to me a feeling of purpose." God, when I'm feeling down about myself and my purpose in life, may I remember to glorify you— that is my purpose!

SEPTEMBER 12

But ask now the beasts, and they shall teach thee; and the fowls of the air, and they shall tell thee.

Job 12:7

Lord, how grateful I am that I once again notice the lovely animals all around me. There was a time in my life when I was so busy, I didn't see them at all, though I know they were always there. Now the birds, the deer—even the raccoons—bring me joy every day as I watch them from my office window. Catching precious glimpses of these creatures of yours helps me value every moment of every day.

For thou art my hope, O Lord God:
thou art my trust from my youth.

Psalm 71:5

Little children automatically see the good
and look for the silver linings. Kids have
such hope built into their personalities. I
recall when I was young, I had faith and
hope that all would be well, even when my
parents or family suffered some illness, job
loss, or other hardship. I just had that seed of
hope in my heart. Now that I am older, I find
my hope in God and his presence and love.
I still feel that sense of goodness and that
all will be well when I am centered in hope
and in him. If I keep my heart open, as I did
when I was little, and come to God for help,
he never fails to give me what I need.

SEPTEMBER 14

Strength and honour are her clothing;
and she shall rejoice in time to come.
She openeth her mouth with wisdom;
and in her tongue is the
law of kindness.

Proverbs 31:25–26

Some chapters in life are more difficult
than others. My mother—who has been a
confidante, a support, and a role model my
entire life—was recently diagnosed with
dementia. Dementia is a long goodbye,
and even as I grieve this loss and help
her navigate a very scary new chapter, I
am determined to remain present for my
husband and our two children. Some days,
I struggle against feeling ground down and
bitter. Many days, I am angry that this
disease is robbing me of my wise mother,
and my children of the grandmother they
have known. God, I am afraid. Please help
me to remain steadfast and honorable in my
actions, no matter what turns life takes
in the days ahead.

SEPTEMBER 15

Thank you for those who pray for me, Father. Thank you for putting me in their hearts and minds. I know that at times someone is keeping me in their prayers, and I haven't the faintest clue. It could be my hairdresser, chiropractor, pastor, or even someone I've just met. Perhaps a checker at the grocery store recalls a bit of conversation we had and now prays for me from time to time. You work in such unusual ways that I never know how it might be happening—I just know that it is so, and I am grateful.

*A friend loveth at all times, and a
brother is born for adversity.*

Proverbs 17:17

Renee's grandmother would say, "Welcome
challenging times, and see who your friends
are." Renee experienced that first hand
when she became caregiver for her ailing
dad. Over time, she learned who thought
of her friendship as a priority: Some
relationships faded because Renee's schedule
was no longer as flexible. It was painful to
realize that not all her friendships were as
close as she'd thought, but looking back now,
she appreciates—and celebrates—the friends
who stuck by her. God, thank you for those
friends who love and support us
through hard times.

And this is the confidence that we have in him, that, if we ask any thing according to his will, he heareth us.

1 John 5:14

Father, teach me to pray according to your will. That's how Jesus taught the disciples to pray: Thy kingdom come, thy will be done. I want to pray like that, with confidence that you hear me and will give me all that you yourself desire. Take away my selfish desires and replace them with your own. Please, Lord, show me what you want. I want to pray for that.

What therefore God hath joined together, let not man put asunder.

Mark 10:9

My wife and I have encountered a rough patch in our marriage. Our youngest child recently began college, and transitioning to an "empty nest" home has been harder on us both than we anticipated. My wife, who misses our sons, has started a new job. She's not home as much just as I've begun contemplating taking early retirement. So many days we seem to be at cross-purposes—we seem to want different things! But this morning when we sat down together over coffee, my wife reminded me that over the years, we have weathered many storms in our marriage—job loss, the deaths of our parents, our middle son's struggles with drugs. Each time we have prevailed together. It was a good conversation, and I think we felt closer to one another than we have in months. Dear Lord, you have joined my wife and me. You have blessed our partnership. To succeed, we must take the long view!

SEPTEMBER 19

As the hart panteth after the water brooks, so panteth my soul after thee, O God. My soul thirsteth for God, for the living God: when shall I come and appear before God?

Psalm 42:1–2

We need water to live, but we often don't think about it until times of scarcity—when we have to monitor its use on a camping trip, or find ourselves under a boil order. Let me not take water—or you, the Living Water—for granted, but offer daily gratitude for this precious resource.

Henceforth I call you not servants; for the servant knoweth not what his lord doeth: but I have called you friends; for all things that I have heard of my Father I have made known unto you.

John 15:15

God wants trusted friends for us. One of the things Cathleen appreciates about her long-standing friendship with Karen is that the two can be open with one another. "I share anything with Karen," Cathleen says. "When I went through my divorce, I was very angry, and Karen was someone I could talk to without censoring myself. She does not judge me. She knows my weaknesses as well as my strengths, and she still loves me!" Dear Lord, may I follow the example of Jesus and share openly and completely with trusted friends.

When Ellie's son Jon was involved in an accident at age 11 that left him with the cognitive functioning of an infant, being his caretaker and tireless advocate became a major part of her life. She changed his diapers, administered liquid food and medicine through his feeding tube, lifted him in and out of his wheelchair, swam with him in a therapy pool, and brought him to church. When Jon died last year, nearly 15 years after his accident, it left a gaping hole in her life. If she was no longer Jon's caretaker, who was she? After her grief subsided, Ellie started making plans for this new chapter in her life. She still advocates for people with disabilities, counsels families in similar situations, volunteers with an organization working with children who have Down's syndrome, and talks about Jon often. "Talking about Jon ensures he won't be forgotten," Ellie says. Lord, when plans change, help us move forward with strength, always seeking out ways to make a difference in this world.

To him that overcometh will I give to eat of the hidden manna, and will give him a white stone, and in the stone a new name written, which no man knoweth saving he that receiveth it.

Revelation 2:17

To those "overcomers" in the church at Pergamos is promised hidden food and a heavenly name. "And thou holdest fast my name, and hast not denied my faith," Jesus says (verse 13). He will therefore feed them with manna, as the ancient Israelites were fed in the desert. He had said in John 6:32 that he himself was the "true bread." But he will also give them a new name. The ancients used a white stone the way we might use a nameplate at dinner, and for the faithful he promises a special place and a special name. To be known by Christ in an individual and particular way was a great comfort to them—and to us as well.

Fear ye not therefore, ye are of more value than many sparrows.

Matthew 10:31

Helen, a 70-year-old widow, stays active and enjoys a wide circle of friends, her two sons, and her grandkids. But sometimes, her body reminds her of the passage of time. "I have a little arthritis," she admits. "Some days it slows me down; it bothers me when I have to ask my kids for help. But then I remember: I'm still me, even with arthritis. My kids love me. And so does God!" Dear God, I am growing older. My body is not as strong as it used to be; sometimes I feel like a burden. But you tell us we are valued, always—please help me to remember this!

SEPTEMBER 24

*And whatsoever ye do, do it heartily,
as to the Lord, and not unto men;
Knowing that of the Lord ye shall
receive the reward of the inheritance:
for ye serve the Lord Christ.*

Colossians 3:23–24

Lord, so often the difference between a productive workday and a fruitless one lies in our attitude. When we truly work as if working for you, it makes such a wonderful difference! Forgive us, Lord, for those times when we dig into our tasks without bringing you into the situation as well. Whether it's peeling potatoes, pulling weeds, or writing a screenplay, we want to tune into your power to perfect our work on this earth.

Teach me, Lord, to look at the world with hope and expectation, not with despair and lack. I am grateful for all you have done for me, but there is still this emptiness inside that catches up to me now and then. Help me see how wonderful my life is, just as it is, and that nothing more is needed to be happy and at peace, for those are gifts that come from within. Teach me to keep my eyes on the bounty that comes from a thankful heart, not from the things we acquire but from the experiences we have and the love we give.
Amen.

SEPTEMBER 26

O Lord our God, grant us grace to desire thee with our whole heart, that so desiring, we may seek and find thee; and so finding thee we may love thee; and loving thee we may hate those sins from which thou hast redeemed us; for the sake of Jesus Christ. Amen.

—St. Anselm

He that hath my commandments, and keepeth them, he it is that loveth me: and he that loveth me shall be loved of my Father, and I will love him, and will manifest myself to him.

John 14:21

When Melanie counseled her 15-year-old daughter, Ella, to reach out in kindness to others, she was thinking of the good Ella might do—and also the way her daughter would benefit. "She's a good kid, but self-absorbed right now," Melanie says. "I want Ella to look beyond herself. She's been feeling bad about herself, and I know from my own experience that by uplifting others, Ella will also feel better in her own heart. I want that for her." Dear God, I honor you when I celebrate and uplift others. I also honor myself. By loving, I become more beautiful and whole.

Rejoice in the Lord always:
and again I say, Rejoice.

Philippians 4:4

Lord, you are the source of all joy!
Regardless of how happy we may feel at any
given time, we know happiness is fleeting.
Happiness, so dependent on temporary
circumstances, is fickle and unpredictable.
But joy in you is forever! And so we come to
you today, Lord, rejoicing in all you were, all
you are, and all you will ever be. Because of
you, we rejoice!

"I have a temper," Therese admits; her short fuse is something she has worked on for much of her life. "I'd been making progress, but then my son Gary turned 15 and we started butting heads all the time!" she shares. "I was discouraged by the setback, but I'm trying hard to respond to Gary in a different, more positive way. With God's help, I know I can continue to grow: as a parent, and as a person."

God, I am a work in progress, and with your help I will continue to grow. Help me to face setbacks in my personal evolution with courage and good humor.

SEPTEMBER 30

Dear God, I ask today for a bold new vision for my life. I ask for the strength and wisdom to be a better person to all those I come in contact with. I ask for the courage to step out of my comfort zone and expand my capacity for joy.

OCTOBER

OCTOBER 1

And moreover, because the preacher was wise, he still taught the people knowledge; yea, he gave good heed, and sought out, and set in order many proverbs. The preacher sought to find out acceptable words: and that which was written was upright, even words of truth.

Ecclesiastes 12:9–10

Father God, please bless our preachers, our pastors, and church leaders. Please give them wise counsel to share with us your words of truth and life. Please keep them strong in their own faith as they foster ours.

A man's pride shall bring him low: but honour shall uphold the humble in spirit.

Proverbs 29:23

Father, it stings when the ones I love correct me. I don't like to be wrong or feel like I'm being criticized. But that's just wounded pride revealing itself. Deep down I appreciate learning the truth so I can learn and grow. Flattery feels nice in the moment, but it doesn't do much real good. People who risk hurting me because they love me are the ones I should listen to. Help me get over my wounded pride quickly and move on in light of what I've learned. And bless those who care enough for me to speak the truth in love.

He that walketh with wise men shall be wise: but a companion of fools shall be destroyed.

Proverbs 13:20

At Kristen's first job out of college, she quickly connected with a group of seemingly fun-loving women. But Kristen soon realized that gossip and drama characterized these friendships, and after some soul-searching, distanced herself from the group. It was only then that she met quiet Amy, a fellow reader who invited Kristen to join her book club. Through Amy, Kristen has met a group of friends who share similar passions and ways of being in the world. Dear Lord, you put friends in my life to guide me. May I surround myself with positive people who help me to grow and be my best self.

OCTOBER 4

By faith Moses, when he was born, was hid three months of his parents, because they saw he was a proper child; and they were not afraid of the king's commandment.

Hebrews 11:23

Dear Lord, my role as a parent puts me in a commanding position. Children have little power, and it is up to me, as my child's guardian, to be a helpmeet and advocate in a world that is not always just. My son, who is nine, has been dealing with a bully at school. I've had to go in to meet with the principal and the other boy's parents several times, and the parents have on more than one occasion grown belligerent. It's an uncomfortable situation, but I know I must remain strong and levelheaded in order to support my child. God, please grant me the strength to always do what is right for my child, even at risk of personal discomfort, as the parents of Moses did.

*Blessed are they which do hunger
and thirst after righteousness:
for they shall be filled.*

Matthew 5:6

There's so much injustice in this world.
There are so many people hurting because
of other people's carelessness, selfishness, or
desire for power and wealth at other people's
expense. Please grant me a giving, generous
heart when it comes to treating people fairly,
to taking care of the widow and orphan, to
welcoming the stranger, and to acting justly.
When it becomes overwhelming, please help
me discern where my efforts can do the
most good in righting wrongs in my social
circles and my community.

OCTOBER 6

They that wait upon the Lord shall renew their strength; they shall mount up with wings as eagles; they shall run, and not be weary; and they shall walk, and not faint.

Isaiah 40:31

O Lord, nothing drains us of our strength more completely than grief. But in times of sorrow, you come alongside us and give us strength to do things we never thought possible. Thus distraught family members are able to make final arrangements, deliver eloquent eulogies, and rise above their grief to do whatever needs to be done. We know that's your strength carrying us in those times, Lord. The promises in your Word give us hope. Your grace abounds in a special way to those who mourn. We praise you for your mercy, Lord. We thank you for your strength.

OCTOBER 7

Lord, a friend was sharp-tongued and impatient with me today. I know she's going through some things in her own life, but it stung! Since it's not like her, do I just let it go? Do I bring it up with her so we can talk it through? Please guide my actions and show me a path forward. Most of all, let me forgive her truly, as you forgive me.

Wealth maketh many friends; but the poor is separated from his neighbour.

Proverbs 19:4

Lord, I live in an increasingly tiered society, in which people associate only with others of similar income. I am grateful to be solidly middle class, with all the opportunity that affords me and my family, and I take pride in my ability to provide for my loved ones. Yet I must remember not to let economics alone inform my relationships with others. The type of car I drive or the size of my home are hollow gauges for who I am as a person; to judge or be judged based on this criteria is not only shallow, but foolhardy. God, help me to remember to choose my friends wisely, honoring the qualities that truly matter— integrity, creativity, wisdom, a sense of justice, and kindness—rather than a person's wealth or status.

*And he saith unto them, Follow me,
and I will make you fishers of men.
And they straightway left their nets,
and followed him.*

Matthew 4:19–20

Jesus, when you call me, let me respond,
like Peter and Andrew, immediately! I get
so immersed in life's minutiae sometimes. I
put off prayer or spending time with you,
because I tell myself that I have just one more
thing that I need to do first. When I feel the
impulse to pray, let me stop where I am and
pray. Let me never forget that before anything
else, I am called to be your follower.

And they that know thy name will put their trust in thee: for thou, Lord, hast not forsaken them that seek thee.

Psalm 9:10

Lord, maybe it's in the times we aren't sure that you are hearing our prayers that we learn to trust you the most. Eventually—in your time—we hear your answer. We know that you are still sovereign, and all our hopes and dreams are safe in your hands. Even when the answer to a prayer is "no," we are comforted by the knowledge that you care about us and respond to our concerns in a way that will ultimately be for our good.

OCTOBER 11

We bring before thee, O Lord, the troubles
and perils of people and nations, the sighing
of prisoners and captives, the sorrows of the
bereaved, the necessities of strangers, the
helplessness of the weak, the despondency of
the weary, the failing powers of the aged.
O Lord, draw near to each; for the sake of
Jesus Christ our Lord. Amen.

—St. Anselm

OCTOBER 12

*They that sow in tears shall
reap in joy.*

Psalm 126:5

I'm an emergency room nurse and love
my job, which can be by turns intense,
interesting, and challenging. No two days are
alike, though much of the time I am invited
to think on my feet. I do like that aspect of
the job. But lately, the ER has been so busy
that by shift's end I find myself exhausted,
both mentally and physically. I must
remember that what I do has value, and
these things run in cycles. I've worked long
enough to understand that the pace will
eventually settle, at least temporarily, and
that I mustn't let a hard day of work get me
down. Dear God, help me to take the long
view. Remind me, on the days when my
spirits and energy are low, that ultimately
things always get better.

OCTOBER 13

As far as the east is from the west, so far hath he removed our transgressions from us.

Psalm 103:12

O Lord, when you promise us you have removed our sins from us, why do we dredge them up so we can wallow in regret and shame all over again? Keep us from wasting time and energy thinking about past mistakes, Lord. If they are no longer on your radar, they surely don't belong on ours. How blessed we are to have such a compassionate, forgiving God!

OCTOBER 14

The way of the slothful man is as an hedge of thorns: but the way of the righteous is made plain.

Proverbs 15:19

Father, I appreciate this encouraging reminder for me to keep chugging along the "high road." When I'm doing the right thing, it can feel like I'm going backwards sometimes—especially when I see others taking not-so-ethical shortcuts and "getting ahead." I confess that when I get tired and frustrated, those shortcuts can look mighty tempting. But taking them would sabotage the good things that are ahead—the good harvest you have in mind for me to enjoy. It's not worth a temporary lapse of integrity for a bit of ill-gained ease to forfeit the fruits of good labor—labor I hope will always honor you.

Give us this day our daily bread.

Matthew 6:11

Thank you for sustaining food, from plain oatmeal for everyday breakfasts to exquisite chocolates for special occasions. Thank you for shared meals with family and friends, where we also share what's going on in our lives. Whatever we eat, ultimately it is your love for us that sustains us.

Truth is a narrow road, and it's easy to fall to one side or the other. For every beautiful kernel of truth, there are a thousand lies that can be made around it. Staying on the straight-and-narrow would be impossible if it weren't for the Spirit of God, who leads us to all truth. Delving into God's Word with the Holy Spirit to guide us is the best way to stay on track and keep walking in the truth.

OCTOBER 17

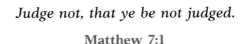

Judge not, that ye be not judged.

Matthew 7:1

Dear Lord, I have a daughter in middle school. She and her friends are coming into their own, trying to figure out who they are. Technology makes it even simpler to be unkind, and it is tempting to adopt a judgmental attitude in order to fit in with others. God, help me guide my children as they navigate this time of change and growth. Please protect my family from the ways of the judgmental, and from adopting those ways in their interactions with others.

OCTOBER 18

The grass withereth, the flower fadeth:
but the word of our God
shall stand for ever.

Isaiah 40:8

Lord, I see you in the beauty of the autumn.
Thank you for the brilliant colors of the
trees. Thank you for the crisp, cool air that
refreshes me. I am blessed to see autumn's
beauty everywhere I go. Thank you for
showing me that a time of change can be one
of the most gorgeous seasons on Earth.

OCTOBER 19

Though he were a Son, yet learned he obedience by the things which he suffered.

Hebrews 5:8

Obedience is a tricky concept. We don't hear as much about it in these modern days! We prize leadership, sometimes at the expense of being a good team member. When I am in a group, at work or at church or at an activity, help me not value leadership so much that I don't appreciate the work every team member does. And when I am in a leadership role, help me remember to be obedient to your will and your words. Let me follow the model of Jesus.

Be strong and of a good courage, fear not, nor be afraid of them: for the Lord thy God, he it is that doth go with thee; he will not fail thee, nor forsake thee.

Deuteronomy 31:6

God, there are times when we must be brave and face an adversary. I work at an ad agency and we are currently bidding on some client work. I'll be making a presentation and competing against rival firms for a lucrative account. Sometimes the competition can get cutthroat. The main challenger has a reputation for badmouthing the competition, and I'm not looking forward to interacting with this gentleman the day of the presentations. God, please strengthen me so that I might face my rival with grace.

OCTOBER 21

May our Lord Jesus Christ be near us to defend us, within us to refresh us, around us to preserve us, before us to guide us, behind us to justify us, above us to bless us, who liveth and reigneth with the Father and the Holy Ghost, God for evermore. Amen.

—10th-century prayer

I will praise thee; for I am fearfully and wonderfully made: marvellous are thy works; and that my soul knoweth right well.

Psalm 139:14

Tabitha's sister Ellen struggles with debilitating shyness. "I try to remember to compliment Ellen sincerely," Tabitha says. "It's very hard for her to socialize with people she doesn't know, and then she gets down on herself. But I tell her, 'You have a tremendous sense of personal style. You are the most interesting-looking person in the room!' I figure, why not remind her of how cool she is? It's true!" Lord, I can help others through praise. May I encourage self-acceptance by building someone else up today.

In every thing give thanks: for this is the will of God in Christ Jesus concerning you.

1 Thessalonians 5:18

It's been a challenging year. I work in a volatile industry, and was laid off after my company merged with another. The layoff came as a surprise, and at a time when my wife and I have been hit with some unexpected expenses, chiefly for home maintenance as we deal with an old roof and an older furnace. And yet, there are blessings. My company gave me a generous severance, which allows me time to figure out next steps for my career without panicking. We have savings that will help us finance the new roof, and I am reminded to be grateful that we have a roof over our heads! Ours is a happy home, filled with children and pets, books and music and sunlight. Dear Lord, even in hard times, there is always something for which I can be grateful.

From personal experience, I think "spilling the beans" sounds too harmless to describe gossip, Lord. I've had so-called "spilled beans" tarnish my reputation, harm relationships, and expose parts of my soul I wanted kept private. But the bright side is that I've learned the importance of finding trustworthy confidants—and of being one. Still, there are times when I'm tempted to talk when I shouldn't or am careless with my "thinking out loud." Help me guard the dignity of those who have confided in me by keeping quiet or speaking only when, how, and where I should.

Ask, and it shall be given you; seek, and ye shall find; knock, and it shall be opened unto you.

Matthew 7:7

Life has made the most hopeful among us skeptical, Lord of truth. Much is bogus, and we are uncertain. Thank you for the gift of doubt, for it sparks our seeking. Keep us lively and excited as we set off on quests blessed by you, heeding your advice to knock, seek, ask.

So the carpenter encouraged the goldsmith, and he that smootheth with the hammer him that smote the anvil, saying, It is ready for the sodering: and he fastened it with nails, that it should not be moved.

Isaiah 41:7

Julie's coworker Greg went above and beyond on a challenging project, and she told him so. Only later did she understand how much her warm words meant: "It turns out Greg was in the process of filing for divorce; he was under a lot of stress, and feeling a little lost personally," Julie remembers. "He told me later that my praise meant a lot during a difficult chapter." Dear Lord, I do not always appreciate what a sincere compliment might mean to someone who needs it. Help me to remember to uplift others at work.

OCTOBER 27

In that he saith, A new covenant, he hath made the first old. Now that which decayeth and waxeth old is ready to vanish away.

Hebrews 8:13

Lord, the familiar is disappearing from neighborhood and nature, and we grieve the loss. Yet, we're resurrection people, unafraid of endings because of the promise of new beginnings. On the other hand, we must learn restraint: Help us, God, to temper our actions with wisdom. Amen.

Ye are the light of the world . . .
Let your light so shine before men,
that they may see your good works,
and glorify your Father which
is in heaven.

Matthew 5:14, 16

Jesus, you said these words to your followers, and they echo down through the centuries to meet me here, as I turn my heart toward you in prayer. As I think of the people you've brought into my life, I think of the times and ways your light has shined brightly through me. I'm also aware of things I do and say, as well as the attitudes I have, that dim or obscure that light at times. Please trim the wick of my words, today; clean the glass chimney of my attitudes; and add the fuel of good behavior to this lamp that is my life in you. I ask these things for the sake of your reputation and to the glory of your Father.

*When Jesus saw their faith,
he said unto the sick of the palsy, Son,
thy sins be forgiven thee.*

Mark 2:5

Jesus, the man who was sick of the palsy
was carried to you by four friends, who very
creatively found a way to lower him from
the rooftop. Thank you for those friends who
carry me to you in prayer when I am at the
end of my rope. Help me to be that
type of friend to others.

A faithful friend is an image of God.

—French Proverb

O God of justice, we confess that we are
too quick at times to judge those around us,
basing our opinions not upon what is written
in their hearts but what is easily seen by our
lazy eyes. Keep us faithful to challenge one
another any time we find ourselves speaking
in generalities about any group of people
or repeating jokes and slurs that offend
and degrade. Remind us that all of creation
bears the imprint of your face, all people are
children of yours, all souls are illuminated by
your divine spark. We know that whatever
diminishes others diminishes your spirit at
work in them. Make us respectful, humble,
and open to the diversity around us
that reflects your divine
imagination and creativity.

OCTOBER 31

Amidst hobgoblins and pranksters, O God, we seek a quiet corner this autumn evening to give thanks for the saints whose day this really is. Be tolerant of our commercialized, costumed hoopla, even as you remind us of the pillars upon which our faith rests today. Keep our trick-or-treating fun, clean, and safe and our faith memories aware, for it is too easy to lose track of what we really celebrate in the darkness of this night.

NOVEMBER

*Open thy mouth, judge righteously,
and plead the cause of the
poor and needy.*

Proverbs 31:9

When Ruth's friend Nora encouraged her
to join in a neighborhood effort to go door
to door and collect canned goods for the
homeless, Ruth was at first hesitant; her
natural shyness seemed to preclude such
activity. But after praying and reflecting on
her fears, she decided to move outside her
comfort zone and help out. The experience
was uplifting: it felt good to be acting—and
speaking—on behalf of those in need. Lord,
please embolden me to speak out for those
less fortunate than myself.

NOVEMBER 2

Lord, how I love to wake up to a cool, crisp
fall day with snowcapped mountains in
the distance and the blue sky above. On
mornings like this I think, what a wonderful
day to be alive! I soon realize, however,
that I should see each day of my life as an
extraordinary gift. Help me to remember to
value each day, Lord. And may I find in each
of them a way to bring glory to you.

NOVEMBER 3

O Lord God, the life of mortals, the light
of the faithful, the strength of those who
labor, and the repose of the dead, grant us a
tranquil night free from all disturbance; that
after an interval of quiet sleep, we may, by
thy bounty, at the return of light, be endued
with activity from the Holy Spirit, and
enabled in security to render thanks to thee.
Amen.

—7th-century prayer

Whoso mocketh the poor reproacheth his Maker: and he that is glad at calamities shall not be unpunished.

Proverbs 17:5

Linda was horrified when her daughter Alyssa and a friend made fun of a man standing farther down the subway platform. "The girls were snickering about his shoes, which were held together with tape," Linda says. "I told them it is never okay to judge those who lack." Years later, Alyssa also remembers the incident. "Mom was gentle but firm: She let me know in no uncertain terms that my behavior was unacceptable. I learned something that day!" Dear Lord, may I live in a way that respects others. May I show by my actions that each person has value.

NOVEMBER 5

And the things that thou hast heard of me among many witnesses, the same commit thou to faithful men, who shall be able to teach others also.

2 Timothy 2:2

Lord, I have the conviction that your presence in my life makes it better: when I let you into my heart, you inform the way I treat others, the way I approach work, the way I move through my days. And good things are meant to be shared! God, help me to share with others the good wisdom I have learned from you. I don't have to proselytize: that's not my style. But through my actions I can demonstrate my beliefs, and in this way create a ripple effect: good begetting good begetting good, with results far beyond what I might even be able to comprehend.

NOVEMBER 6

For he hath not despised nor abhorred the affliction of the afflicted; neither hath he hid his face from him; but when he cried unto him, he heard.

Psalm 22:24

When I am feeling uncertain and alone, I can turn to the scriptures. The prophets often felt unworthy of their call. Hannah felt alone in her barrenness. Jesus himself cried out on the cross, quoting Psalm 22, asking why God had forsaken him. But God's love reached all of them.

The hope of the righteous shall be gladness: but the expectation of the wicked shall perish.

Proverbs 10:28

I see people every day doing wrong and bringing harm to others, and benefiting from it. I see good people suffering and losing everything, and I wonder where the justice is. Lord, help me remember your justice happens on a much higher level and that the hope of the good is always rewarded, while the motives of the evil are always judged and accounted for. Let me not have any expectations that come from a place of selfishness or greed, but help me, Lord, to always hope to be my best, and do my best, for myself and others. If I walk the right path, I may still suffer, but I know my ultimate reward will be joy. May I always walk the right path, Lord.

Now in a song of grateful praise,

To thee, O Lord, my voice I'll raise:

With all thy Saints I'll join to tell,

My Jesus has done all things well.

And above the rest this note shall swell,

This note shall swell, this note shall swell,

And above the rest this note shall swell,

My Jesus has done all things well.

—Samuel Medley

NOVEMBER 9

*I can do all things through Christ
which strengtheneth me.*

Philippians 4:13

Eli was born with severe developmental
issues, and his childhood has been a journey
of acceptance, hope, and courage on the
part of his parents, Joyce and Ron. "We
didn't anticipate having a child with the
challenges Eli faces," Joyce says simply. "But
he is an amazing person. And God is there
for our family. With God's help, Ron and I
have tapped into strengths we didn't even
know we possessed to help our son reach his
potential." Dear Lord, help me to tap into my
inner spiritual reservoir for strength. I know
that strength is there! I know you are there!

He who trusts himself is lost. He who trusts
in God can do all things.

—Alphonsus Liguori

NOVEMBER 10

Every man according as he purposeth in his heart, so let him give; not grudgingly, or of necessity: for God loveth a cheerful giver.

2 Corinthians 9:7

My wife is a nurse, and lately the hospital where she works has been short-staffed. Though new hires will soon be brought onboard, for the time being, my wife's schedule is more taxing. When I promised her I would pick up the slack at home, including taking on more of the cooking and cleaning, I was sincere. And yet, yesterday I was tired and ungraciously reminded my wife of all I was doing. Her face fell, and I was ashamed; here we are, both working so hard, and I spoiled my kind efforts with bitterness! I have since made amends, but dear Lord, please remind me to give with good cheer, not grumbling.

Blessed are the pure in heart:
for they shall see God.

Matthew 5:8

When I read this beatitude, I think of my
grandmother and her warm, radiant smile.
Though she was a busy woman with a
number of hobbies, she spent time in prayer
every morning and every evening, and
that prayer time was her spiritual anchor.
More than that, when she saw something
beautiful, she spontaneously praised God.
When something good happened, words
of gratitude sprang from her lips. What a
beautiful example she was, of someone in
tune with God's will.

*Faithful are the wounds of a friend;
but the kisses of an enemy
are deceitful.*

Proverbs 27:6

When twelve-year-old Maren found herself
suddenly courted by the "cool girls" in her
middle school, she began to ignore an old
friend, Lily. Lily called her out on it, but
Maren's new friends laughed and said Lily
wasn't worth Maren's time. Feeling torn and
unhappy, Maren talked to her mom, who
encouraged her to talk to God; in the quiet
of home and prayer, Maren saw the situation,
and her steadfast friend, with clarity. Dear
God, a good friend lets us know when we've
done wrong. May I be open to words of
constructive criticism, shared by those who
love me; may I see false platitudes
for what they are.

Be careful for nothing; but in every thing by prayer and supplication with thanksgiving let your requests be made known unto God.

Philippians 4:6

I am the single mom of two teens. The last year has been challenging for me as a parent: My daughter has had a hard time adjusting to the rigors of high school academics, and my son has been testing boundaries when it comes to curfews and expectations at home. Some nights I am troubled by insomnia, and then the next day, I have a shorter fuse. Tempers flare. Dear Lord, please help me to remember that you are there for me. You are the answer to my anxiety. Help me to parent with wisdom and rely on you, even when I feel stressed and uncertain.

NOVEMBER 14

There's an old joke that it's easy to love your neighbor in church, but it gets much harder in the church parking lot! Lord, I'd like to ask you to be with me today and every day when I spend time in transit. Whether I'm dealing with rude drivers or inconsiderate fellow commuters, let me be loving and forgiving, and dial down the road rage—or even just the "road irritation."

This is the day which the Lord hath made; we will rejoice and be glad in it.

Psalm 118:24

Precious Lord, forgive me for the habit of labeling my days as good or bad. For I know in my heart that there is no such thing as a bad day. Every day you create for me is a gift. What I experience during the duration of it is neither good nor bad, but what you planned for my enjoyment or my growth. Help me begin each day believing that it will be a joyful day with you, Lord. And when I close my eyes at night, may I rest knowing that, no matter what transpired, it was a very good day, and tomorrow I will rejoice and be glad in it!

NOVEMBER 16

Thus speaketh the Lord of hosts, saying, Execute true judgment, and shew mercy and compassions every man to his brother.

Zechariah 7:9

We live in an information society. Daily, we are bombarded with news. Our phones, televisions, and laptops keep us breathlessly apprised of the latest events. It is good to be informed, and technology is a gift. But an adverse effect of all-information-all-the-time is a sort of numbing of the senses. "Another earthquake?" we shrug. "Another tragedy?" It can be an effort to dig deep and access caring, and yet compassion is a Godly virtue. God wants us to experience concern for the sufferings of others. Dear Lord, help us to strike a balance in our information intake so that we retain compassion for those in need. May we never become callous to others' misfortune.

NOVEMBER 17

Now therefore ye are no more strangers and foreigners, but fellowcitizens with the saints, and of the household of God.

Ephesians 2:19

In my house, things usually work best for everyone when we all pitch in and work together. In the house of God, we must be of service to one another in the same spirit. We may be strangers in one sense, but in another we are interconnected and we share a fellowship around our love of God and our desire to do his will. Let us all learn to work together in service to the whole, because when the whole is happy, every individual benefits. God, help us to think not just of ourselves and our own needs, but the needs of our families, our communities, and our planet.

NOVEMBER 18

A man's gift maketh room for him, and bringeth him before great men.

Proverbs 18:16

For years, Nancy worked in a job that, though lucrative, left her feeling emotionally empty. When she turned 40, she decided to make a change. Though she had no children of her own, she had often been told she had a gift with kids, so she returned to school and earned a teaching degree. Today, she teaches biology to middle schoolers. "It felt like a risk to make such a big change, but I've never been happier!" she shares. God, you have blessed me with gifts to achieve great things. Please help me to discover these gifts and use them.

Judge not according to the appearance,
but judge righteous judgment.

John 7:24

Those people who are unlikable to me, Lord,
are not worthless, though I'm tempted to
believe my self-centered thoughts about
them. Rather, Lord, these people are
precious works of beauty, created by you.
And if I bother to look beyond my first
impressions, I will be delighted by what
I see of you in them.

For where two or three are gathered together in my name, there am I in the midst of them.

Matthew 18:20

Lord, how comforting it is to know that you don't require large numbers of people to come together in order for you to be present. So often it's in the spontaneous coming together of two individuals who turn their hearts toward you that your presence is felt most clearly. Thank you for taking time to meet with us, Lord. May you always feel welcome.

O Lord, we give thanks for your presence, which greets us each day in the guise of a friend, a work of nature, or a story from a stranger. We are reminded through these messengers in our times of deepest need that you are indeed watching over us. Lord, we have known you in the love and care of a friend, who envelops and keeps us company in our despair. When we observe the last morning glory stretching faithfully to receive what warmth is left in the chilly sunshine, we are heartened and inspired to do the same. When we are hesitant to speak up and then read in the newspaper a story of courage and controversy, we find our voice lifted and strengthened by your message in black-and-white type. Lord, we are grateful receivers of all the angelic messages that surround us every day.

O God, the light of every heart that sees thee, the life of every soul that loves thee, the strength of every mind that seeks thee, grant me ever to continue steadfast in thy holy love. Be thou the joy of my heart; take it all to thyself, and therein abide. The house of my soul is, I confess, too narrow for thee; do thou enlarge it, that thou mayest enter in; it is ruinous, but do thou repair it. It has that within which must offend thine eyes; I confess and know it; but whose help shall I implore in cleansing it, but thine alone? To thee, therefore, I cry urgently, begging that thou wilt cleanse me from my secret faults, and keep thy servant from presumptuous sins, that they never get dominion over me.

—St. Augustine

And Saul said to David, Thou art not able to go against this Philistine to fight with him: for thou art but a youth, and he a man of war from his youth.

1 Samuel 17:33

Kevin has always thought outside the box; now he's graduated university and is in the process of starting his own business. It is an exciting time, but he gets discouraged by the doubt some friends express about his venture. "Remember the story of David and Goliath," his mother tells him. "David succeeded against all odds. Don't let doubt stop you from achieving your dream!" Dear Lord, Saul doubted that David could overcome Goliath. But David did not let a doubter—and a powerful one, at that!— stop him from one of his greatest life achievements: defeating Goliath. God, when others doubt me, may I draw strength from David's story.

He causeth the grass to grow for the cattle, and herb for the service of man: that he may bring forth food out of the earth.

Psalm 104:14

The bread is baking in the oven, and our home smells wonderful. Thank you for the pleasure we take in the process of baking, the anticipation as we wait for the result, and the nourishment this food will offer.

NOVEMBER 25

O Lord, as we enter this season of thanksgiving, how important it is for us to grasp the concept of "enough." You know how this world tempts us with all that is bigger, better—more in every way! But there is such joy and freedom in trusting that you will give us exactly what we need—neither too little nor too much. May we never take for granted all the blessings we have, Lord, and may we be as generous with others as you are with us. It is the simple life that brings us closest to you; we are blessed when we live simply.

NOVEMBER 26

Dear God, from whom every family receives its true name, I pray for all the members of my family; for those who are growing up, that they may increase in wisdom and love; for those facing changes, that they may meet them with hope; for those who are weak, that they may find strength; for those with heavy burdens, that they may carry them lightly; for those who are old and frail, that they may grow in faith.

—Anonymous

*To the end that my glory may sing
praise to thee, and not be silent.
O Lord my God, I will give thanks
unto thee for ever.*

Psalm 30:12

Lord, so often it isn't until after a crisis has
passed that we can see all the ways that
you were present in the midst of it. Forgive
us for focusing on the negative and missing
your positive contributions. Remind us to
expect your involvement—to actively watch
for it, even! We need to be alert to the
working of your Spirit in all things and
give thanks at all times.

NOVEMBER 28

I will instruct thee and teach thee in the way which thou shalt go: I will guide thee with mine eye.

Psalm 32:8

Enid's faith helps her as she pursues the dream of opening a bookstore. "I've wanted to run a bookshop since I was little," she says. "I used to go to the independent bookstore in my hometown; it was an important place in my childhood. Now I'm opening my own shop, in the town where I went to college." Is she scared? "Sometimes," she says. "But I feel like God is guiding me in my decisions. That gives me courage." Dear Lord, thank you for guiding me as I dream of great things.

Two ears, one mouth? Perhaps a hint, subtle or not, about what is more important in life, Great God. Make me at least as ready to listen as I am to talk. Give me patience to listen to the concerns, the hopes, the dreams of these important people called family, for that is how we connect. There are times to talk and times to listen. Please help me to know the difference.

NOVEMBER 30

Above all, taking the shield of faith, wherewith ye shall be able to quench all the fiery darts of the wicked.

Ephesians 6:16

Today I face a frightening health issue, God, and I am more afraid than I would like to admit. Nobody wants illness. Nobody wants to go under the knife or be told they may not live to see their children grow up. But I have you, God, and with your presence today, I know I can get through any challenge. I know I can stand up to the fear and the worry and vanquish it with love and faith. I know you don't give me more than I can handle, God, and that you'll be there to handle it with me nonetheless. Thank you, God, for being my shield and my rock and my faithful warrior.

DECEMBER

DECEMBER 1

And all things, whatsoever ye shall ask in prayer, believing, ye shall receive.

Matthew 21:22

Prayer, O God, is as steadying as a hand on the rudder of a free-floating boat and as reliable as sunrise after night. It keeps me going, connected as I am to you, the source of wind beneath my daily wings.

DECEMBER 2

Therefore the Lord himself shall give you a sign; Behold, a virgin shall conceive, and bear a son, and shall call his name Immanuel.

Isaiah 7:14

O Lord, what a blessing to be entering the Advent season and prayerfully considering the joyous celebration of your birth. Don't let us get so bogged down by minutiae that we miss the miracle, Lord. Prepare our hearts as we prepare our homes and families for Christmas, and help us keep our focus not on everything we need to do, but on you.

DECEMBER 3

God is our refuge and strength, a very present help in trouble.

Psalm 46:1

You give your help, O Comforting God, not in proportion to our merit, but based only on our need. For you come not only to those who are "keeping it together," but to those of us who are fragmented and fractured. I need the tenderness of your caress so that I know I am not alone in my awful feelings of weakness.

DECEMBER 4

Stand in awe, and sin not: commune with your own heart upon your bed, and be still.

Psalm 4:4

Lord, it's wearying trying to be on the cutting edge, working to "be somebody," scrambling to get to the top of the mountain first. Sometimes I need to pull away from the rat race and be quiet; to put away my goals, appointments, and lists and just be with you, Lord. I crave the peace of your presence, and I need to feel held by you. Please pick me up and let me lean against your heart, which I know is full of love for me and all the world.

DECEMBER 5

I have shewed you all things, how that so labouring ye ought to support the weak, and to remember the words of the Lord Jesus, how he said, It is more blessed to give than to receive.

Acts 20:35

I am grateful for the blessings in my life: a strong marriage, good health, and a steady job. I firmly believe that these advantages put me in a position to help those less fortunate than myself. On a fundamental level, I think that's why we're here—to assist others. But some days I do grow weary of the work constant service (either service I've elected to do or that which has been thrust upon me) requires. On those days, God, please help me to remember how giving fills one spiritually. Christ taught that it is better to give than to receive; please help me to remember this on the days that I struggle.

DECEMBER 6

Blessed are the meek: for they shall inherit the earth.

Matthew 5:5

Please grant me a listening spirit. With my spouse, my children, my friends, let me be someone they can approach with problems and questions, knowing I will be gentle with them. Let me be appreciative when I hear others express wisdom and insight, rather than always having to be the person to have the answers myself. And when I am called to lead, let me lead with love and a listening ear to the concerns of others.

DECEMBER 7

And Joshua said unto them, Fear not,
nor be dismayed, be strong and of
good courage: for thus shall the Lord
do to all your enemies against
whom ye fight.

Joshua 10:25

God, teach me to not fear adversity. It is a
mother's kneejerk reaction to protect her
children from all trials, but one cannot travel
through life without reversals of fortune.
Help me to accept and face challenges not
only to myself but to my children. My
kids will face unkindness; they will face
unfairness, loss, and even cruelty in their
life's journey. God, help me to remember that
adversity breeds character—that we cannot
necessarily control what happens to us but
we can control our response to it. Grant me
the strength to respond to adversity with
grace, and please guide me as I give my
children the tools to greet life's vicissitudes
with faith in you, and with courage.

DECEMBER 8

A new heart also will I give you, and a new spirit will I put within you: and I will take away the stony heart out of your flesh, and I will give you an heart of flesh.

Ezekiel 36:26

O Lord, who hast mercy upon all, take away from me my sins, and mercifully kindle in me the fire of thy Holy Spirit. Take away from me the heart of stone, and give me a heart of flesh, a heart to love and adore thee, a heart to delight in thee, to follow and to enjoy thee, for Christ's sake.

—St. Ambrose

DECEMBER 9

Come now, and let us reason together, saith the Lord: though your sins be as scarlet, they shall be as white as snow; though they be red like crimson, they shall be as wool.

Isaiah 1:18

On laundry day, as I'm removing stains that have been allowed to set, I remember this verse. Thank you for the power of your forgiveness. Please let me turn to you in repentance as soon as I've done something wrong, not allowing that sin to set and deepen and become habitual.

DECEMBER 10

Let nothing be done through strife or vainglory; but in lowliness of mind let each esteem other better than themselves.

Philippians 2:3

I was proud when my middle-school son participated in a local speech competition recently. He placed well in the district levels, and will be moving on to compete at the county level. The county level, of course, will feature winners from other districts. All these kids will be "cream of the crop," which means that the competition will be stiffer. The event takes place next week, and my son is a little nervous about how well he will place. What if he does not get as high a ranking at the county level as he did at the district level? My wife and I have counseled him to just try hard, enjoy himself, and never lose sight of the difference between healthy competition and destructive rivalry. Dear Lord, thank you for guiding my son and his peers to respect one another as they strive to do their best.

DECEMBER 11

And when Peter was come down out of the ship, he walked on the water, to go to Jesus. But when he saw the wind boisterous, he was afraid; and beginning to sink, he cried, saying, Lord, save me.

Matthew 14:29–30

Jesus, sometimes I see your presence so clearly in my life, and it is easy to walk towards you. But then I lose my focus and take my eyes off you, and begin to sink back into old habits and old sins. During those times when I cannot walk towards you in confidence, let me cry out, like Peter, for you to save me.

DECEMBER 12

And Moses called unto Joshua, and said unto him in the sight of all Israel, Be strong and of a good courage: for thou must go with this people unto the land which the Lord hath sworn unto their fathers to give them; and thou shalt cause them to inherit it.

Deuteronomy 31:7

Gina's mother, Olivia, had always been the matriarch, the "glue" that held her family together. When Olivia was diagnosed with Parkinson's disease, Gina, as the eldest of her siblings, knew she needed to step up and be strong for everyone. "I suddenly was called upon to mediate and make decisions that affected the entire family," Gina remembers. "It was ultimately a time of growth, but I felt challenged. I prayed for guidance a lot." Dear God, please embolden me to be a leader, just as Moses uplifted Joshua to lead the Israelites into the promised land.

DECEMBER 13

Today, in the dreary days as we head toward winter, I celebrate flowers. How wonderful it is to see their bright colors. I am grateful for the chance to bring flowers into my home to brighten a dreary day. Thank you for the colors and smells of spring and the opportunity to welcome them into my life at any time of year.

Think not that I am come to send peace on earth: I came not to send peace, but a sword.

Matthew 10:34

Lord, I have a difficult decision ahead of me. Deep down, I know what the best and most righteous course of action is. But I'm letting myself second-guess myself, pointing out that other reasonable, well-meaning people are choosing the easier path and are able to justify it to themselves. I find myself hoping that outside circumstances will change before I have to commit to the right course of action and alienate some friends. I wonder why I have to be the one to summon up the courage to do right. Please grant me that courage.

DECEMBER 15

Lord, I feel angry at so many people. Often I think my life would be peaceful if only they would just do the right thing. I convince myself they are robbing me of peace, but at this moment I know it's my choice to let go of anger and embrace peace. Staying angry at them for not living up to my expectations doesn't solve any problems—it just creates new ones. Please help me to remember that anger does not bring about the righteous life that God desires—in me or in those I'm staying angry at. Give me strength to release them—over and over again if need be—so I can go back to that serene, tranquil place called "peace." In Jesus' name. Amen.

And Elijah said unto Elisha, Tarry here, I pray thee; for the Lord hath sent me to Bethel. And Elisha said unto him, As the Lord liveth, and as thy soul liveth, I will not leave thee. So they went down to Bethel.

2 Kings 2:2

God gives us strength to go with our friends and share their burdens and responsibilities. When my friend and mentor, Diane, needed to travel to a cancer clinic in another city, I felt called to accompany her. I could not change her diagnosis, but I could be there, as a friend and companion, as she has been there for me these many years. Dear God, thank you for the powerful gift of friendship. May I tap into your strength to be steadfast and true to my friends; as Elisha accompanied Elijah, may I walk beside my friends in good times and bad.

DECEMBER 17

Therefore, as ye abound in every thing, in faith, and utterance, and knowledge, and in all diligence, and in your love to us, see that ye abound in this grace also.

2 Corinthians 8:7

At work, Ann has composed a crack team of motivated, talented people; she's not afraid to push these colleagues to reach their maximum potential. But she's also very aware that the tone she sets is key. "It's okay—even desirable—for me to push everyone around me to greater heights," she shares. "But it's imperative that I be kind about it." Dear Lord, when I push others to succeed, may I be kind!

DECEMBER 18

Lord, sometimes I feel guilty that I haven't thanked you enough for the blessings in my life. I know I possess luxuries that others merely wish for. In this cold month of December I am grateful for the roof over my head, the heated seats in my car, and the warmth of my family and friends. Remind me not to take these kindnesses for granted and help when I see someone in need.

DECEMBER 19

Though I speak with the tongues of men and of angels, and have not charity, I am become as sounding brass, or a tinkling cymbal.

1 Corinthians 13:1

An important part of Violet's job is motivational public speaking, which requires a lot of energy. "Sometimes I get fatigued," she admits. "But I try to tap into the love I feel for my audience—and when I look out from the stage, I do love these people! That love inspires me and gives real meaning to the work I do. People sense my authenticity and respond in kind." God, may I do what I do with love and attention!

DECEMBER 20

Then said Jesus unto his disciples, If any man will come after me, let him deny himself, and take up his cross, and follow me. For whosoever will save his life shall lose it: and whosoever will lose his life for my sake shall find it.

Matthew 16:24–25

A few days after retiring, Nancy visited the local hospital and asked how she could be of service. Her kids were grown, and she and her husband had divorced a decade ago. She wanted to define a new way to make a difference. "My volunteer work fulfills me," she says now. "I feel I am manifesting Christ's teachings when I help others; serving God in this way helps me realize my best self." Dear Lord, may I always remember that self-realization is achieved through my service to you.

DECEMBER 21

And he turned him unto his disciples, and said privately, Blessed are the eyes which see the things that ye see: For I tell you, that many prophets and kings have desired to see those things which ye see, and have not seen them; and to hear those things which ye hear, and have not heard them.

Luke 10:23–24

Give us eyes with which to see, noses with which to sniff, ears with which to hear the faintest sound along the paths you have set for us, O God of Daily Joys. Following you is a whole experience—body, mind, and soul.

DECEMBER 22

You are a welcome guest at this table, God,
as we pause in the midst of this bell-ringing,
carol-making season of too much to do. Send
us your gift of silent nights so that we can
hear and know what you will be bringing
us this year: yet another gift of hope. Bless
our gathering around this table; we will set
a place each day for you. Join us in our daily
feast, for which we now give thanks.
May it nourish our busy bodies as the
anticipation of your presence among us does
our weary spirits.

DECEMBER 23

For God so loved the world, that he gave his only begotten Son, that whosoever believeth in him should not perish, but have everlasting life. For God sent not his Son into the world to condemn the world; but that the world through him might be saved. He that believeth on him is not condemned: but he that believeth not is condemned already, because he hath not believed in the name of the only begotten Son of God.

John 3:16–18

O holy Child of Bethlehem,

Descend to us, we pray;

Cast out our sin and enter in.

Be born in us today. Amen.

—Traditional prayer

DECEMBER 24

Tangled in tape, lists, and holiday wrappings, we are all thumbs of excitement! Bless the surprises we've selected, wrapped, and hidden. Restore us to the joy of anticipation. We want to be surprised, too. Our wish lists include the gift of peace possibilities, of ears to hear a summons and eyes to spot another's need or triumph, of being able to make a difference. As we cut and tape, God of surprises, remind us to keep in touch with the gift's recipient after the wrapping papers are long gone and the ornaments packed.

DECEMBER 25

Joyful all ye nations rise,

Join the triumph of the skies;

With the angelic host proclaim

Christ is born in Bethlehem.

—Charles Wesley

Compassionate and holy God, we celebrate
your coming into this world. We celebrate
with hope, we celebrate with peace, we
celebrate with joy. Through your giving
our lives are secure. Through your love we,
too, can give love. You are the source of our
being. Joy to our world.

DECEMBER 26

Lord, we want to live life to its fullest.
And although we know we shouldn't place
our own wants before others' wants, it
is so easy to think our dreams for the
future matter most. Remind us to make
compromises. Our love can get us further in
this life than selfishness.
Amen.

DECEMBER 27

Teaching them to observe all things whatsoever I have commanded you: and, lo, I am with you always, even unto the end of the world. Amen.

Matthew 28:20

How can I be lonely in a crowd? But sometimes I am. Let me see those feelings of loneliness and restlessness not as bad things that I must try to escape, Father God, but as sensations that lead me to retreat and seek your presence. You are my peace and my hope, and only in you can I find rest.

DECEMBER 28

Then Eli answered and said, Go in peace: and the God of Israel grant thee thy petition that thou hast asked of him. And she said, Let thine handmaid find grace in thy sight. So the woman went her way, and did eat, and her countenance was no more sad.

1 Samuel 1:17–18

Lord, I know how Hannah felt. She took her struggles with infertility to you in prayer, and "poured out [her] soul" to you passionately and honestly. Witnessing her, Eli misunderstood, thinking she was drunk. But when they talked, he displayed your compassion to her and relayed a promise, and Hannah went away trusting in your promise.

I am sometimes more skeptical than Hannah, Lord. Please grant me the grace to trust that my struggles are witnessed by you, and that you care for me and have the best path for me in mind.

DECEMBER 29

Scooting over to make room, God of daily bread, the kids and I greet you over our peanut-butter-and-jelly lunch. Bless this, our favorite feast. Through simple graces to bless childhood fare and bedtime prayers to offer you the day, I'm honored to introduce you to my child. But how can I explain who you are to such a little one as this?

Why did I worry . . . again a little child is leading. You are, as played back in toddler chatter, simply "dear God." An understanding wise enough to last a lifetime.

DECEMBER 30

Lord, as I clean out closets and make lists for the New Year, show me any "gods" I have placed before you. Help me to look honestly at how I spend my time and my money. Does one of these areas of investment reveal a strong allegiance to something other than you? If so, Lord, help me eradicate those distractions from my life once and for all.

DECEMBER 31

Our light affliction, which is but for a moment, worketh for us a far more exceeding and eternal weight of glory; while we look not at the things which are seen, but at the things which are not seen: for the things which are seen are temporal; but the things which are not seen are eternal.

2 Corinthians 4:17–18

Whatever trouble this year has held, it has only been momentary. God has been working in you something eternal and unseen, a brightness and splendor beyond your comprehension. It is the full weight of his glory. Don't dwell on the details of this last year's failure or loss. Instead trust God's work; he is preparing you for an eternity with him.